Lacanian Psychoanalysis from Clinic to Culture

This accessible and insightful book merges Lacanian theory, psychoanalytic case studies, and the author's personal experiences to illuminate the relevance of Lacanian psychoanalysis in mapping contemporary subjectivity.

Using examples from cinema, artificial intelligence, and clinical and cultural references, the book covers major topics within the field, including dreams, the mirror phase, psychosis, hysteria, the position of the analyst, the drive, supervision and the symptom. Each is set within the context of our technologically oriented, market-based society and complemented with empirical vignettes. The book's final section examines contemporary society and radicalization.

Lacanian Psychoanalysis from Clinic to Culture is important reading for students and academics in Lacanian psychoanalysis, as well as professionals concerned with complex social problems.

Berjanet Jazani is a medical doctor and a practising psychoanalyst in London. She is the Honorary Secretary of the College of Psychoanalysts and a member of the Centre for Freudian Analysis and Research.

The Centre for Freudian Analysis and Research Library (CFAR)

Series editors:
Darian Leader, Anouchka Grose, and Alan Rowan

The Centre for Freudian Analysis and Research (CFAR) was founded in 1985 with the aim of developing Freudian and Lacanian psychoanalysis in the UK. Lacan's rereading and rethinking of Freud had been neglected in the Anglophone world, despite its important implications for the theory and practice of psychoanalysis. The CFAR Library aims to make classic Lacanian texts available in English for the first time, as well as publishing original research in the Lacanian field.

Lacanian Psychoanalysis from Clinic to Culture
Berjanet Jazani

Lacan and Marx
The Invention of the Symptom
Pierre Bruno
Translated by John Holland

The Law of the Mother
An Essay on the Sexual Sinthome
Geneviève Morel
Translated by Lindsay Watson

Lacan Reading Joyce
Colette Soler
Translated by Devra Simiu

Obsessional Neurosis
Lacanian Perspectives
Edited by Astrid Gessert

The Marks of a Psychoanalysis
Luis Izcovich

For more information about this series, please visit: https://www.routledge.com/ The-Centre-for-Freudian-Analysis-and-Research-Library-CFAR/book-series/ KARNACCFARL

Lacanian Psychoanalysis from Clinic to Culture

Berjanet Jazani

Routledge
Taylor & Francis Group

LONDON AND NEW YORK

First published 2021
by Routledge
2 Park Square, Milton Park, Abingdon, Oxon OX14 4RN

and by Routledge
52 Vanderbilt Avenue, New York, NY 10017

Routledge is an imprint of the Taylor & Francis Group, an informa business

British Library Cataloguing-in-Publication Data
A catalogue record for this book is available from the British Library

Library of Congress Cataloging-in-Publication Data
A catalog record has been requested for this book

ISBN: 978-0-367-33094-1 (hbk)
ISBN: 978-0-367-33092-7 (pbk)
ISBN: 978-0-429-31797-2 (ebk)

Typeset in Times New Roman
by River Editorial Ltd, Devon, UK

For B. and my Mum:
My two confidantes.

Contents

Acknowledgements

This book is the result of one single moment: a moment of disbelief. Faced with total despair, I chose to believe in life, love and light out there, somewhere. Therefore, I am most grateful for all the unconditional, nurturing love I have received since then and forever, which has maintained my belief in possibility and in change.

I wish to express my sincerest respect to each and every single one of the people with no name who generously contributed towards that moment. And, to the suffering of all my beloved ones to which this is the least that can be said.

I wish to thank everyone within or associated with CFAR. To all CFARians: first and foremost, to trainees and students; to founders and teachers; to all affiliate, associate, analyst members; to all artist, academic, translator, editor and writer friends of CFAR; to Ethics, Training and Management committees; to clinicians at our low-cost clinic; to CFAR Journal and Library contributors and, last but not least, to Pat Blackett. You all have created a "home" faithful to the soul of analysis and research.

To my most-difficult-to-work-with patients and analysands, who do not hesitate to constantly challenge my knowledge and experience.

To my much-loved victims: my students and my readers.

To all of my teachers and supervisors from medical school in Tehran, and to Dr Abdi Rafatian.

To my editors: Rosanna Hildyard and Julie Scrase.

To rock and jazz music. Specially, British hard rock and metal, which made this land a "hope" for me many years ago!

To Disney and Pixar animations, which were most inspiring to my writing.

And, finally to the scent of spring, summer, autumn and winter in my *Iran*. I count the days until I can once again feel the passage of time in the lands of Phoenix.

Foreword

I strongly identified with the opening chapters of this fascinating book since they reminded me of my childhood in Communist Yugoslavia, where the regime, similarly to the Iranian regime, regarded psychoanalysis with disdain and Freud's books were hard to find. Berjanet Jazani shows how in a situation where people experience limits in their pursuit of knowledge, desire to learn and understand becomes even stronger than in places where these limits do not exist. This desire to know and understand became, in Jazani's case, the driving force in her decision to become a psychoanalyst.

As a child, Jazani was taken both by knowledge that she found in the encyclopedia and questions that have been raised in Freud's *Interpretation of Dreams*, which was her mother's favorite book. When Jazani made a change in her career and instead of following a secure path of practicing medicine embarked on a curvy road of training to become a psychoanalyst, it was as if she was drawn by the unknown, which the knowledge offered in the encyclopedia and the medical books could not explain, which is why she started pursuing psychoanalytic studies abroad.

Jazani intertwines her personal memory of her childhood and university years in Iran with the theoretical reflections she developed as a practicing psychoanalyst in the UK. In analyzing the relationship between a child and a mother, she makes an important observation on how a mother's way of treating language plays a fundamental role in the child's positioning in relation to the mother's own lack. While psychoanalysts often speak about the problems children have with mothers who do not speak much to the child, Jazani astutely observes that talking too much might be equally problematic. Mothers who cannot stop talking might prevent children to find their own position in language. As a result, such children have problems forming their own desire. There is a strange silence related to the talkative mother – on the one hand is the silence of her jouissance, in which the child remains stuck, and on the other hand is the silencing power of her relentless chatter that she imposes on the child.

Jazani's analysis of psychoanalytic cases will be of great help to anyone who wants to understand the premises of the neo-liberal ideology of success and the symptoms people form in the context of its pressures for perfection.

Jazani offers examples of how people interpret their parents' ideas of what is a perfect image and how neurotics and psychotics differently relate to the presumed gaze of a caregiver. While neurotics might constantly deal with the dissatisfaction in regard to their image and also question the desire of the caregiver, some psychotics might find strange reassurance in the imagined gaze of the caregiver. One person, for example, was able to function only by way of daily visiting his mother's place. Even when his mother died, this man continued with his ritual since he needed the imagined gaze of his mother. This ritual allowed this man to function and when the arrangement he had with the imagined mother's gaze collapsed, he entered psychoanalytic treatment.

Jazani's presentation of cases allows us to understand the value of psychoanalysis for people who try to come to terms with their daily life problems as well as with their past. One patient, for example, wanted to remember her past in order to be able to lead a carefree life. In analysis it became clear that "carefree" was actually meant as "free of care". As a person who was recovering from addiction, the patient was constantly controlled by her father and her desire to remember her past was linked to her attempts to form her own solutions to her problems and not be constantly under the care of her caregiver.

A large part of the book deals with the complicated subject of remembering and forgetting. Jazani explains with great theoretical rigor how neurotics and psychotics differently deal with remembering. For a psychotic subject remembering can be especially painful. However, what is hard to deal with for one person might be pacifying for another. An example can be a person's uneventful past. For one person, this might be appeasing, but for another, it can be unsettling. Equally, for some psychotics, the moment when they "find out" what has happened in the past can present the moment of crisis, while for others it might offer a new meaning, which helps the person to hold himself together. Jazani in a similar way shows how creativity can play very different roles in people's lives. While a manic depressive might want to use art to make great impact in the outside word, a psychotic can use art as a safe space with the help of which he can interact with other people.

The concluding parts of the book offer interesting insights into how new technology is used and interpreted differently for people who have neurotic or psychotic structures. For one psychotic patient, a commercial genetic test provided the means for coming to terms with questions about paternity. While the person did not find his actual father, his condition stabilized when he found the information about his ancestry. The very fact that he was able to trace back his line of ancestors allowed this person to find a solution for the traumatic fact that he did not know his father. Other psychotic patients found help in their mobile devices and apps. When these people tried to perform their daily tasks, these devices functioned like a crutch that allowed them to stabilize their condition and hold themselves together. There are, however, also people for whom new technology offers a way through which their delirium gets channeled. It is not unusual that a person feels that all kinds of haunting messages are being transmitted to him through computers and mobile phones.

Jazani's book makes a trajectory from her life in post-revolutionary Iran to her life ina world dominated by artificial intelligence, genetic tests and mobile devices. The opacity of the regime that she was dealing with in her past has allowed Jazani to observe the opacities that are at the core of new technologies. In addition, Jazani offers an insight into how this new technology is reshaping today's subjectivity and how psychoanalysis can be of help to people whose symptoms are also altered in our technology-driven world.

Renata Salecl

The journey begins

If someone had told me, many years ago, that I would write a book in the future, I would certainly have laughed. "That's not something I want to do," I would have replied, sure of myself. I was always much more of a reader and talker than a writer. I started teaching when I was 12. That summer, I was preparing to bypass the first grade to go straight on to the third grade in secondary school. I had started to study the second grade by myself, earlier that spring. Later, in the chapter "A resident of the world", I will explain why I was in such a rush to finish school but I am sure that I was enjoying the mood and the pace. Closer to the exam date, in early September, I enrolled for maths class for a period of two weeks. This class was actually for those who were repeating the second year – they disliked me very much. Yet, I was drawn to volunteer my services to them: to teach, while learning with them. And so we became friends!

I enjoyed the experience to the extent that I decided to work as a private tutor from that point. Now, looking back, I think that what I found attractive about teaching was in stimulating thought in my victims as much as in facing the challenges brought upon me while transmitting knowledge. As a result, I was always inventing new ways and methods of teaching. But all the way through, writing was completely alien to me. Writing was equated with storytelling, or, to be more precise, with concocting a story. It was not serious enough to do as a job, or even, perhaps, as a project that has turned into a vocation. I think I can now acknowledge the fact that I had tamed and squared myself into different boxes and masquerades. Medicine is the most obvious example, and sometimes I still miss it, I must admit. However, what I do not miss about it is the endless repetition of true/false and the pattern of "proven/not enough evidence". The whole market and politics at play in this field disappoints me.

The mission of a particular desire, the desire not to know, acts in fact as a defence or perhaps protection against an unruly, wild drive. A desire – always in disguise – manifested once I found myself treating the condition of a student of mine, rather than teaching her. This young student had learning difficulties. Her much older parents had employed me to help her with maths and science. In my first visit to her, she was indifferent to my presence and all my attempts at communication failed. The only child of her parents, there was a 60-year age difference between her and her father, and 45 years with her mother. As a benevolent gesture, her parents had decided to buy her a kitten, so that she could resolve her communication difficulties with others around her, including them. However, all the chores of owning a pet were done by her mother; my student had not even named her kitty. Besides this, her science teacher at school wanted the class to give an oral presentation. My student could not face the idea. Now, looking back, I seem to have been more interested in the cause of her difficulties than in training or teaching her how to present in front of her class or to please her teacher. I remember making innovations in my teaching strategy, for example, by buying her little cacti – her favourite plants – every week, and encouraging her to name and take care of them. Through this nurturing act, I also encouraged her to decorate her shelves in the way she wanted to. I was lucky to have her mother to back up my mode of intervention. My student started to talk to me and was happy enough to play me some of her favourite music on her computer. We both had an interest in Iron Maiden! I introduced Jimi Hendrix and Dire Straits to her and she was eager to convince me that Queen was cool too.

After a few weeks, with a shelf full of cacti, music in the air and a kitty on her lap, her father came into her room after returning home early from his work trip. Well, he found nothing of the teacher–student scenario that met his expectations. I was fired and not paid. Her mother reached out to me a bit later, to send me her gratitude for making her daughter more sociable, and her regret about the fact that her daughter's grades in science and maths were not impressive at all. I also received a note from my student saying: "Rock rocks!" with a little heart in the corner. I could not have been more pleased.

Indeed, her "rock" rocked something in me too. I just needed a good few years to act upon my desire to teach, as well as work on my relationship with the ivory tower of knowledge. In a way, the question I needed to target was: what was the effect of such an intervention and at what level? What purpose could different kinds of creative acts serve and, as a result, what could be transformed? It is not always humour that transforms a tragedy, and why transformation in the first place? Where can a desire be detected? I did not just want to be blinkered by the correct knowledge. I wanted to search for it endlessly, while questioning it at the same time.

Thanks to Freud's Irma dream, the field in which to work through this desire was made available for me to discover, years later. While writing the first chapter, I rediscovered the excitement of his first discoveries for myself, through the realisation of his endeavour to push beyond available facts and theories. I admire his courage in sharing his difficulties and understandings through his practice. In fact, the very essence of Freudian psychoanalysis is the underlying belief in sharing our ignorance with each other, driving the windmill of exploration to keep turning. Desire speaks out in many different ways.

The story behind the chapter "A black swan in the mirror" begins with my own preoccupation with the role of Captain Von Ebrennac in Vercors' short story, *Le Silence de la Mer*. His magical power to break the silence! Initially,

I had decided that the chapter title should be "Le Silence de la Mèr(e)". My patient's case history, however, got in the way of my choice of title. I wanted to express something about maternal love in the French language. I could not help being reminded of the soul of resistance in France during the Second World War and was unable not to think of my mother's enduring love for her children. I am also conscious of the experience suffered by some, of lacking such a love. And yet this does not mean that one does not search for it in the hope of finding it, locating it, somewhere, at some point. Our desire to love/be loved is beyond any imposed circumstances.

I wrote the "*Memento*" chapter in order to express my appreciation to all my psychotic patients who taught me and reminded me that there is a non-pathological approach to the lives of patients. Over the past two decades, they have transformed my unconscious stigmatising. I had enjoyed watching the movie *Memento* in the early 2000s, several times. However, I was not, at this point, employing the clinical approach I currently use with psychosis. And yet, my medical mind was not quite satisfied with my understanding of Leonard's condition either. My analysis of his condition is indebted to one real-life psychotic subject. The movie's release date was around the time that the "bipolar" diagnosis was being found everywhere, to the extent that I wanted to be checked for it too. So, I appointed one of my psychiatrist professors at the time. I seemed to tick all the boxes but I was not yet convinced – based on their regimental diagnostic method – why, then, I was exempt!

"Inside out?" is a response to the dogma of current attitudes towards the human subject in our contemporary time. This attitude affects human society on many levels: from politics, to market economics, education, and – more relevantly – the question of so-called "mental health". The chapter is an expression of angry disagreement with such reductive thinking. On a brighter note, this chapter and the next one, "Founder and inventor", are results of my experience with the clinic of neurosis in this country. This is where I started out with my psychoanalytical practice. For this chapter I am very grateful in particular to the resistance of a certain case of obsessional neurosis, which is where my innovative side kicked in.

"Is singularity near?" is not a reactive piece, as it might seem to be. Rather, it is a construction based on the fieriest stimulating debates with my husband Ben during early-morning walks in the park. It was only hypoglycaemia that could make us shut up, and then the rush to work at breakfast time made us forget about the topic until the next morning, for a good few months one spring. At last, he got some idea of the drive and I had to admit my – slightly – hypocritical approach to new technologies. I can smell lattes even now, while remembering that period. I got the debate out of my system and I am very hopeful to advance our arguments at some point with other adamant researchers of the psyche and AI.

Another door was unlocked for me when I became suspicious about the agency of medical care while treating a patient who was close to the end of her life. I would also later find an annoying tremor in my hands while operating under the supervision of an expert surgeon. I consulted a neurologist. "No organic cause found": this paved my way and directed me to my first analyst's consulting room. I had lost all the confidence I held in medical science, as well as my approach to the suffering of patients. The tears of that patient will always be remembered.

Yasmin Levy's music has alleviated some of the most painful moments in my life. As much as the texture of her voice is a remedy, it is associated with a rather significant shift in my destiny as a psychoanalyst. Her *La Juderia* reminds me of my own home before a self-imposed exile. A home at the end of a close, from which I have one last photo: two suitcases in an empty salon. I appreciate my new home and I am well aware of the fact that some breakdowns on the road can potentially prompt a transformative process. It certainly did in my journey. My supervisors were not my mentors; rather, they were my most serious critics, to whom I owe finding my way back, as well as remaining my models for an ethical position towards my patients and analysands. They were definitely not the kind, affirmative listeners that my beloved grandmother was. Many years later, after the breakdown on that motorway, I saw an image of it sent to me for an art project. I did not recognise the route of my old commute; nor did I recognise myself, back then.

Reminding myself not to enjoy too much the suffering induced by being a resident far, far away from the lands once called "home"; reminding myself to not get too used to the current circumstances; ideas of how history marks a subject and how s/he relates to it – these are explored in the chapter called "A resident of the world". The subject's own power, which can have a transformative effect, goes beyond any phallic measurements. One cannot be totally carefree about the aftermath of a historical event. However, a subjective history does not follow the same law of linear time. The urgency is to a moment of subjective conclusion. Through the work of analysis, this is exactly what we push a subject through; to arrive at a testimonial state. Many psychoanalysts agree on this point, which is referred to as one possible "exit" from analysis.

In the last chapter, we explore the trade-off between a perverse politics and psychotic discourse in the social trends of today. Psychoanalysis is a product of a culture, created by a subject of desire and drive. Historically, it is known for its interest in ideologies, religions and social tragedies such as war and revolution. Recent memories of the catastrophes resulting from radicalism, terrorism and war require a complex analysis that goes beyond the available explanations, which often only duplicate facts and hence create more, repetitive vicious circles.

As I began this part of my book with a transformative moment of conclusion, I would like to end with a promise of hope. A hope that is nurtured with care and love. Through small vignettes, I have told you stories of my life from the past up until now. Like the idea of sharing and transmitting knowledge in psychoanalysis, our testimonial is where we find the subject who speaks. I have already detected the trace of at least two of my desires here while addressing something to you: the faces of desire. Firstly, I discovered how much I would like to write rather than teach. It was through writing this book that I got a chance to explore more "how" and "what" to address to the others through writing. I also questioned my style of narration through this experience which I hope will be elaborated in my future writings.

My second desire refers to the questioning and researching about available concepts in the field of psychoanalysis. Through different chapters, I have tried to re-learn and re-think the psychoanalytical approach to the subject's suffering and challenges. I had initially considered a different title for this book: "*Phoenix: Faces of Desire.*" The myth of Phoenix has a significance in Persian art and literature as much as it does in my personal history. It represents a rebirth as Phoenix arises from the ashes of its predecessor. We can think of the relation between the meaning of such a myth and the concepts of "symptom" and "desire" in Lacan's work. After reworking some chapters, I realised that this book is rather a testimonial journey through some of Lacan's theories. It is a souvenir, or a memento, of my own journey. Although this book is a collection of essays on Lacanian concepts which I have learned from both psychoanalytical literature and the clinic, I do hope that it will not be treated only as a means of transmitting a knowledge of psychoanalytical theories. Rather, I hope that it acts as an agent to stimulate and challenge your unconscious: my dear reader.

At the end is love and only love …

London
October 2018

Chapter I

I have a dream ...

My story with Freud's work

Before the invention of search engines, before the creation of new, epic information technologies which made all knowledge accessible at a click away, there was
a book called an encyclopaedia: grandfather to Wikipedia. It was a magical
moment, to go to it and find there a new detail about Greek mythology, or the
name of the capital city of any country in the world. In fact, these two areas were
my obsessions, researched and searched for over and over again in that hefty,
dusty book on the shelf. It was the book that acted as my means of travelling and
excavating; in fact, I would later learn that these were Freud's two well-known
passions.

This book was my *agalma*; the object of my transference to knowledge. It
had it all, and hence became a reliable means of compensating for the answers
others failed to give. "Go and check it with the E-so-pe-da!" I used to insist,
whenever someone hesitated over answering. I cannot pinpoint the exact date
at which the book became the means of compensation, backup or guarantor of the
Other's lack or shortcoming, but it was my buddy, I guess, from the age of four.
It was – obviously – read aloud to me in those days, until I was confident – perhaps too much so – to tease my classmates by snubbing them over ridiculously
unnecessary, boring and nonsensical information about, for example, the date of
birth of a certain inventor in the eighteenth century.

There was, however, one other book of equal significance: *The Interpretation of
Dreams* by Sigmund Freud. I owe my obsession with this one to my mother. Not
for nothing did she spend hours with her head in her copy while keeping an eye
on me playing around with my little sister. She had a great respect for that book.
It was her favourite, and so I badly wanted it to be read to me. "No!" she said.
Now, remembering my earliest memories from those days, it seems, strangely
enough, to have been her encyclopaedia. Every single time that my sister had a
tantrum (or I had provoked her into throwing one) my mother turned back to
that book. At least, that was how I interpreted this parental course of action with
regards to the omniscient reference book. I am not sure what she was searching
for in those pages discussing dream wish fulfilments, hysterical patients'

symptomology, transference and resistance, the origins of neurosis, etc. – nothing there to be found on parental guidance – but her symptom became my destiny.

Before jumping forward in time to my life events of 23 September 2003, I want to tell you the story of my first, and quite traumatic experience of reading Freud's book for myself. I read: "... dreaming of a dead mother is a wish for one's mother to be dead." Immediately, anguish and guilt haunted me. I had had numerous dreams in which my mother was dead and from which I woke up in a terrible state of anxiety, searching for her.

During the first few years of my childhood, Iran was undergoing radical socio-political changes. My mother, my infant sister and myself were dependent only on each other and, of course, books were, therefore, the primary stimulant to my imagination. It is no wonder, then, that the two aforementioned books were more like people than objects to me. The Freud book was as much of a rival for my mother's attention and her desire as my infant sister was – I hated them both! (My sister knows, of course, how much I love her.) There was also the occasional call from my father to punctuate our week, his voice coming down the phone from far, far away each Thursday, somehow setting an awareness of the time of week into my head. The actions of psychoanalysts, listening and occasionally talking, remind me of those Thursday scenes. Interestingly enough, the very first words I learned to communicate with were: "forbidden" and "Thursday". Both were intertwined with each other in different ways: from the aftermath of the 1979 Revolution in my home country, which made the presence of the father into the voice of Thursdays; to the presence of the forbidden book (of Freud) taking up the Other's desire. Both were associated with the symbolic law of the father operating at the level of my mother's desire.

The forbidden book of my childhood is the book of Freudian psychoanalysis. It was the culmination of the last decade of the nineteenth century. Fifteen years after the "Caesar of Salpêtrière" (Charcot's) Tuesday lectures in Paris, the outcome of ten years of observation and experimentation with patients and five years after Freud's famous dream of Irma, *The Interpretation of Dreams* was published.

This book, which was written in the very last year of the nineteenth century, but was dated to the first year of the twentieth in order to be the book of the century, is Freud's most ground-breaking work, as he himself referred to it later in life. It is the result of all that formed Freud as a psychoanalyst; Freud's sinthome. He invented methods of listening, talking and (hopefully) curing which go beyond hypnotherapy or any other cathartic method. He had devised his own method of therapy. The full account of Freudian psychoanalysis is found in this book. Later works of Freud were focused on developing and modifying what he had discussed there, but *The Interpretation of Dreams* is what Freud is known for, as the founder of psychoanalysis.

23 September in the mid-1980s

On the first day of autumn, 23 September, sometime in the mid-1980s, we were to start school. This was the most celebrated day of the year for me, for many years to come. Unlike many who find the start of school in autumn a real disaster after summer life, I was over the moon and could not wait to see "the world". Admittedly, going to school – back then, in the context of post-revolutionary Iran – meant checking in to a prison of radical religio-ideologisms. However, for those of us who were hungry to learn, even this atmosphere had little effect. It was unfortunate to learn later in life that this date on which we started school actually coincides with the anniversary date of Freud's death.

I had decided to pursue a medical career even before starting the school. My maternal grandmother had predicted a bright future for me in which I was apparently supposed to "wear white". My unconscious had interpreted her equivocal suggestion as a reference to a doctor's white coat: therefore, to becoming a medical doctor. Later I learned that, in fact, my mother also wished the same profession for me; and furthermore, I was aware that my father never got the chance to finish his medical degree. I knew of his wish to become a practitioner of the "talking cure"; however, he also had a high admiration for surgeons. Therefore, my early wish was to become a surgeon. The result of an unfinished task of a parent, further to an understanding I had taken from an ambiguous prediction, decided my symptom formation: to be a medical practitioner, particularly, a surgeon.

I was raised by two women for the first five years of my life: my mother, with strict rules and discipline; and my grandmother, with supportive love and the language of poetry. Looking back to those early years, starting at the school did not only represent liberation from maternal jouissance; education was also absolutely necessary to me in order to accomplish my mission in life. Becoming a doctor meant studying at school. Learning at school became an enjoyment parallel to my fantasising about a different world outside our household. In the autumn of the mid-1980s, my curiosity about my mother's private time with Freud's book eventually found relief. A super-religious teacher, whose mission in life was the inquisition and brainwashing of my generation, disclosed to us that Freud was a deviant thinker whose immoral, perverted thoughts paved the way for sexual freedoms all over the world. We were advised to avoid any contamination from his ways, and report anyone from our family who advocated Freud's so-called cult. I did not report my mother's preoccupation with Freud's work to our teacher. Was the forbidden book of my childhood also forbidden for the rest of the world? I wondered.

Only a few weeks into my first year at primary school, Tehran suffered under heavy bombardment during attacks in the Iran–Iraq war. Schools were closed down and we were home-schooled by educational TV programmes. In my eyes, this was a disastrous event: forced back home again! I remember the nasty war from this perspective at the level of two drives: a restriction on seeing the world (scopic drive), and intimidating noises coming from a grey sky (invocatory drive). I found the new situation of being home-schooled more tolerable with the help of my school uniform. By the time each TV lesson began, I had my full school uniform on, and never failed to pretend to have my classmates around me. I occasionally talked to my imaginary teacher and schoolfriends. My mother later told me that she became really concerned when, on one occasion, I had apparently pretended to have a fight over a lost pencil with my imaginary friend sitting next to me. This also shows how badly I wanted to leave the maternal nest.

During my teenage years, the loud background noise of the war was replaced by the sound of hard rock and metal music, while the fantasy of travelling the world had given up its place in my heart to motor sports – I still cannot express how much I enjoy my time around car engines and learning about the restoration of classic cars. I finished secondary school and sat for the university entrance exam two years earlier than the usual time of graduation, at the age of 16. I simply could not wait to start studying medicine. I gave up on all my leisure activities: on literature and history books, rock music and sport cars. I had actually learned to drive early on, but as an inexperienced driver I was in a couple of bad car accidents and, lesson learned, sophisticated medical school was all that I needed to tame my passion for fast-paced adventure. Before medical school, my boyish hobbies used to surprise my friends. I did try to change myself a bit – by learning about classical music and ballet, poetry and meditation. However, despite appreciating these new sources of enjoyment, deep down I remained always more interested by those of my teenage years. However, for the most part, medicine consumed all of my time, to the extent that having a quick lunch during anatomy class was not unusual. The early years of medical school passed quickly. I preferred studying the French approach to medicine, rather than the American medical training that has been taught in Iranian medical school for many years. Why I preferred the French approach to medicine was not down to any reason in particular other than that it carried the significance of being "French". This association with the "French" signifier, similarly to my rather "boyish" interests and hobbies ("boyish" according to stereotypes at the time) seemed to be relevant to my first name. My father had gifted me with a name that sounded French to native speakers of Persian and his inspiration had its origin in a similar name for boys. Well, I may have studied American medicine but later I went on to study the theories of the French Lacan. Of course, it was more than just an Imaginary identification to my first name that led me to become a psychoanalyst. Later in this book, I will explain more about my journey of becoming an analyst.

My years in medical school were divided between theoretical courses and the internship in training hospitals. The first moment I really found myself suffering during my medical training was in the dissection room during the anatomy course when I was 17. I admit that such an encounter with a human corpse can be a shocking moment for many who study medicine. Later, in my personal analysis, I realised I had made an association between the man's life-less body that lay on a metal bed before me and the loss of the grandfather to whom I was so close. Both the loss of him and watching the illness from which he eventually died left a mark on my unconscious. For many years, even after finishing my medical degree, the nightmare of that dissection room still haunted me. The marks left by some events in the early years of my life – both at the level of language and the body – were later revealed and elaborated upon during my analysis. My unconscious fantasy of curing an illness or help-ing someone who suffers from a malaise had its root in the loss of my beloved grandfather. Furthermore, some of the bodily symptoms and illnesses I have suffered from seem to be related to my grandfather's type of illness. Not much longer after this in my childhood, my other grandfather suffered a paralysing stroke and was suddenly bedridden for the rest of his life. I was truly in agony during my training rotation from the neurological wards to the Intensive Care Unit. This other grandfather was rather more of a playmate to me, possessed with a great passion and knowledge about cars. His affliction made my child-hood years prior to primary school go suddenly silent but his passion spoke out not only through my interests in motor sports and car engines but also in the formation of my symptom of moving from place to place.

The second time I found myself once again feeling alienated from the prac-tice of medicine was during my internship in hospitals and Accident & Emer-gency. I felt unreasonably anxious delivering my duties on shift and on more than one occasion my supervisors had to remind me that my role was that of medical practitioner, not social worker. It was sometimes impossible for me to separate the two positions, which was eventually explored in analysis. On one occasion, I was assisting our professor while conducting surgery on a termin-ally ill patient with a malignant melanoma. While receiving anaesthetic, the patient said in tears that she feared for her two children's future after she was gone. I was the worst assistant that my professor could have had for that long operation that lasted seven to eight hours. I was so preoccupied with what she had just articulated that my hands had a terrible tremor. This moment in my medical training made me question for the first time whether I should become a surgeon. Later, the effect of her words – both on my mind and on my Real body, such as the tremors in my hands – was explored in detail in the analytical space. It decided my current position as a clinical practitioner: as a psychoanalyst rather than a surgeon.

My "symptom" of becoming a doctor during the course of analysis eventu-ally gave way to the formation of a "sinthome", which was writing. A symp-tom that once caused me a great deal of malaise underwent a sea change. I shall elaborate on my experience of writing on a later occasion as I am just at the start of this journey. But the status of my symptom changed absolutely into something that involved the constant, creative actions of researching, chal-lenging and analysing thoughts and ideas. I had a dream (of becoming an assistant doctor) which went through a kind of dissection itself. The dissection of the Real symptom – which ex-sisted the Symbolic – provided the material with which to construct my sinthome of "writing".

23 September 2003

The forbidden Freud does not only concern the laws of certain states; psycho-analysis as a method of research and treatment has been a target of ignorance and misinterpretation in so-called "mental health". From "pop" psychoanalysis to "exclusive" psychoanalysis at the level of theory and practice, whatever it is that is referred to as psychoanalysis is often quite different from Freud's hard and lifelong work.

I started my private practice on 23 September 2003, receiving my first patient in the early days of autumn in that year. He was tormented by obses-sional thoughts of his wife's unfaithfulness. My very first supervisor was a psychiatrist with no knowledge of any talking cure: a highly-recommended doctor, with a lengthy list of patients in a training hospital: "He has OCD and needs a kick-start of a moderate to high dose of Clomipramine." My experimen-tal mind wanted to listen to my patient's narrative about his symptomology. I privately appointed another supervisor, who was faithful to Melanie Klein. She suggested a type of listening and interpretation for treating that case, which I then combined with my knowledge from Freud's book. While the above aids helped reduce my anxiety, they did not seem to have a particular effect on the patient's prognosis. After a couple of months of treatment, having compared my patient with the many others in the hospital clinic with the same diagnosis, I was struck by the clear differences between each case of supposed OCD. The limitation that faced me was the start of my formation as an analyst in later years. Becoming the clinician I wanted to be was an aim that could not possibly be achieved through any knowledge transferred from an academic form or through a handbook. Although I studied Freud's book on the excavations and discoveries of the 1890s, it certainly did not shape me to become what I am now. It would perhaps be best if Freud's work was treated as something to learn on the way to fuller knowledge, as well as being a kind of "work in progress" itself – an investigation of a method which continues to be investigated beyond Freud's own time.

If the contemporarysocio-political circumstances in Iran had not been quite so imposing and restrictive (particularly to women), I am not sure if I would have chosen a self-imposed exile in London. I am sure I would certainly have searched outside Iran for further training; my personal story testifies to it. However, it is more likely that I might have returned to somehow conclude my journey there.

When I visited No. 19 Berggasse in Vienna for the first time, strangely I did not have the feeling of being in the master's home. Rather, I wondered what I would have become as a subject – a subject after undergoing analysis – if Freud had not moved there, to then break up with Joseph Breuer. It seems to have been a move to a new city which was carried out with great hope, passion and the ambition to create and found something. A family home in harmony with the culture he grew up in, the school of psychoanalysis was to be formed within the circle of family members, connected by friendships. It is also heartbreaking to think of Freud leaving that safe corner after 47 years to go into exile, and yet, on to a productive last year of life. Although it is rather strange that the date of Freud's death is coincidental with significant dates at the start and throughout my journey of analysis, it is certainly not the expiry date of Freudian psychoanalysis. After all, we do not believe in a start and end as such in psychoanalysis today. We work in a tradition, which was taken up from where Freud himself had sensed a need for further elaboration: he had run out of time and another fresh start was to come and continue to uncover the great mysteries of the human psyche. Saadi Shirazi, a Persian poet, once said: "There is no end to a man of noble actions; what is remembered will keep him eternally alive."[1]

23 September 2018
London
To the memory of my Grandfathers

Note

1 This line of poetry was engraved on my grandfather's tombstone by an anonymous person. At the time of writing the piece, this memory was not present in my thoughts. However, it occurred to me – surprisingly – at the end of my presentation in a seminar held by CFAR.

Chapter 2

A black swan in the mirror

The mirror phase theory

A few years ago, I received an individual who was trying out every possible treatment and solution so as to become the best ballet dancer in an upcoming show. She was a young woman, the only child of her mother, and whose father was never known to her. She was well educated and from a wealthy family, seeking psychoanalysis through her mother's recommendation alongside yoga, Pilates and t'ai chi. She believed that equilibrium is reached through investing in both mind and body.

Psychoanalysis, as seems to be true for many other patients, was reduced to a "mind spa" for her. Disentangling her mother's demands from her own was the first and the most difficult task at the beginning of the treatment. The mother was so involved in her daughter's daily life that it was almost impossible to distinguish the one from the other. The patient did not seem to be bothered by this situation, unlike many others who are eager to keep a distance from the mOther.

I intervened as early as the first meeting, when she wanted to pay me through her mother: "you don't pay your fees yourself?" She seemed struck by my question. The effect of my intervention was not only the content of my sentence but also the way in which it was addressed to her. She had the option of taking responsibility. A space was given to her to do so. The next session, she said that she had never thought about taking charge of her bills and expenditures. Even for her daily expenses, she had her mother's credit card while her own income was her "saving for the future" as per her mother's advice. However, she did want to try this option – which had up until that point been so alienating for her – of paying me herself. This was the point from which the work started. Psychoanalysis, which was reduced to a "mind pacifier spa", did not remain at this level and became instead an ally to the patient creating her private space. For those who have watched it, it is almost inevitable that we are reminded of the Darren Aronofsky film *Black Swan*.

Nina Sayers, the main protagonist, did whatever it took to perform her best and to attain "perfection" as a ballet dancer. In the film, the presence of mirrors, perfectionism/narcissism and the mother and daughter dyadic relationship is too focused on the "here and now" for us to know much about Nina's child-hood. However, it does not take a lot to guess her mother's total dependence on her. Her omnipresent gaze is everywhere, a constant intrusion. Her gaze is not situated in the symbolic position of the third element in the mirror phase; rather, it is looking through the eyes of the specular image itself.

The aggression and absolute narcissism in Nina's life are well depicted in this film. Lacan referred to the formation of the ideal ego as a result of the child's reaction to the mother's omnipotence in his Seminar 4 (Lacan, 1956–7). The ideal ego of the Imaginary order includes an anticipation on the side of the child of becoming "such and such" in the future. What fails to take place here is the passage from an absolute narcissism/perfectionism to the formation of the sub-ject's desire. This passage is from being an individual to becoming the subject of desire (Lacan, 1966a). The I/ego is formed but subjectivity itself will not get a chance to burgeon (Lacan, 1953–4). Nina has not identified with her mother's desire but simply copies her. The ideal ego in the realm of the Imaginary for Nina is to become the star of her dancing group. This is her ultimate goal and compass in life, leaving nothing beyond that. This pattern is well illustrated during the final scene and in her final words: "I did my best performance."

The subject's position never had the chance to be taken up and lived through. The image in the mirror, which often gets mixed up with her real body as well as that of her friend, gets transformed and disintegrates. The image, as she imagined it for herself to present to all the little others – her mates and her coach – is the one that she is in love with, being the white or black swan of the troupe. The dual-ism in which she is entangled moves from one extreme to the other: from white to black swan, from good to bad girl. This spectrum is a pattern often observed in the clinic of schizophrenia.

Paranoid thoughts and delusions are part and parcel of the dualism between an omnipotent mother and the child from which a symbolic space is foreclosed. Nina's wish to be "the one" or to become "the one" coincides with Freud's theory of desire or more precisely of wish fulfilment (Freud, 1914–1916), rather than with what Lacan formulated as the desire of the subject in the Real. Her tendency and wish to become "the one" stays in the Imaginary realm. Although Alexandre Kojève, a French Hegelian philosopher, distinguishes the ego/I from the cognitive/thinking I of Descartes, influencing Lacan as early as the mid-1930s, nevertheless Lacan's conceptualisation of the desiring subject moved away from Kojèvian desire (Roudinesco, 2001).

My patient also had an omnipotent mother from whom she had never been sep-arated. When the earlier history of the case became clearer in the work, all the parental settings and strategies seemed to have created a physical and practical separation in her daily life. For example, she had never spent a single night in her mother's room or been physically attached to her. In earlier vignettes from her childhood, what seemed to be absent was verbal *communication* between the mother and child. The mother was highly educated and a university lec-turer. The act of speaking was domineering in the household in which my patient had grown up; the mother was a non-stop speaker, leaving no space for interruption. The more material arose from her childhood, the more the key element of the Symbolic in the act of speaking was missing. The realm of spoken words had remained at the level of description and explanation, a translation of cognitive meaning. If a caregiver occupies the position of an instructor and the mother–child relation revolves around dos and don'ts, there will be no place for a possibility of a Symbolic space beyond such a dyadic relation. There will be no relationship as such. Furthermore, the position that the child takes up will not be separated from the Other. However, this does not place the blame with the caregiver. It simply provides potential material for the child to remain entangled between the Imaginary and Real. The Lacanian *méconnaissance* should not be taken as misunderstanding but as an alienation from the Other of the body and language. This non-stop speaking is then equated with an empty speech which is reduced to a vehicle of meaning. We can call such non-stop speaking of the mother the "silence of the mother", a mute and opaque jouissance in which a child remains stuck. The child does not find a position in language to take it up independently from the Other, a position from where the subject's unconscious interprets a Symbolic lack in the Other based on which she can form her own desire. Furthermore, if such a Symbolic position is not facilitated for a child and she only learns how to speak her mother tongue – like a learned skill – the law of the Symbolic will not be transmitted to her through language. A mother's way of treating language plays a fundamental role in the child's positioning in relation to the mother's own lack. Her own submission to the Other's law changes her omnipotent presence for a child. Instead, such a lack allows for a child to take up a position and form a desire and a symptom. We learn from Lacan's later teaching that a subject's unconscious interprets her mother tongue's equivocation to form a symptom which will ultimately separate her from the maternal jouissance. It is again a subject's own responsibility to interpret an equivocation in her mother tongue to form a symptom. The paternal metaphor, in fact, facilitates and finalises this process of symptom formation.

As the support of the Imaginary for each subject originates from the mirror phase, both Nina Sayer and my patient's confidence and self-image were constantly doubted. The mother's own exaggerated omnipotent image of self was at stake instead of the child's image in the mirror phase. Moreover, their perfectionist mothers had put an impeccable ideal ego (being the best dancer or performer) before their children. Whether it was a case of an imposing mother or the child's interpretation of her mother's standards for a perfect image, the result was a subject engulfed in the Real of maternal jouissance with a problematic support of the Imaginary at the level of both meaning and self-image.

The genesis of the mirror phase theory

The inception of Lacan's theory of the mirror phase dates back to the mid-1930s. The first draft of this paper never had the chance to become available and was doomed to be erased from the history of conceptualisation of the mirror phase due to an interruption in the 14th IPA (International Psychoanalytical Association) conference in Marienbad during August of 1936. This was the first time Lacan presented a research paper on psychoanalytical theory at an international psychoanalytic conference. The trace of thoughts found in the published version of the 1936 paper can be found in the 1949 article, thirteen years later when Lacan was more famous within and outside France (Lacan, 1966b).

Ernest Jones, the chair of the IPA panel, interrupted Lacan a few minutes after starting his presentation. Time at the conference was limited and each speaker was allotted a fixed amount. Lacan was not famous in the psychoanalytic world at that time and was only a member of the SPP (La Société Psychanalytique de Paris), a small group of psychoanalysts in Paris. He was known in Paris but mainly in the fields of philosophy and literature. In response to this interruption by Jones, Lacan went to Berlin to watch a sporting event organised by the Nazis and held at the Berlin Olympiad (Roudinesco, 2001). He was a young 35-year-old man soon to become a father – his first wife was pregnant at the time – and he had a passion for Freud's ideas and for philosophy. Linguistics was a great source of interest to him. According to Élisabeth Roudinesco, Lacan does not chronologically belong to the first generation of psychoanalysts after Freud, which was mainly concentrated in the German speaking world; nor is he of the second generation. Due to his renovation of psychoanalysis, Lacan belongs to the third generation after Klein and Winnicott.

The concept of the mirror phase, introduced by Lacan in this paper, was initially a subject of experimental tests and a paper by French psychologist, Henri Wallon, in 1931. However, Lacan made reference only to James Baldwin and never mentioned Wallon throughout his works on the image and the mirror (Borch-Jacobsen, 1990). Wallon had described human infant and chimpanzee reactions to their own reflection in the mirror at around the age of six months. This was considered as a psychological developmental stage under the name of "mirror test research". Wallon, in his book *The Origins of the Infant's Character*, focuses on the child's behaviour in relation to his mirror image and environmental elements between the ages of six and eighteen months old. He also refers to the idea of unifying the body in this experience (Wallon, 1983).

Besides Wallon, René Zazzo, another French psychologist, had also conducted experiments regarding the infant's experience of the mirror and had outlined four developmental stages undergone by the infant in response to his own reflected image (Zazzo, 1948):

a)   recognising the other's image
b)   taking his image as another child
c)   recognising the specular image
d)   identifying with the image

Roudinesco in her book *L'analyse, L'archive*, gives us a historical account of the mirror phase theory. Furthermore, she refers to the influences coming from other schools of thoughts and expertise into Lacan's approach to the concept of the mirror phase. According to her, at the time of writing the 1936 paper Lacan was familiar with Françoise Dolto's ideas and was an eager reader of Alexandre Kojève, a French Hegelian philosopher. Indeed, he co-authored an essay with Kojève under the title of "Hegel and Freud" in July 1936 – one month prior to his Marienbad presentation. The essay included three parts: 1) the genesis of self-awareness; 2) the origin of madness; and 3) the nature of the family.

The thread of thoughts and concepts can be found throughout Lacan's works between 1936 and 1949. Some of the ideas in the 1936 paper were published in a 1938 paper called "Family complexes in the formation of the individual" before being presented in 1949 at the 16th IPA conference in Zurich. The first English translation was done by Jean Roussel and the paper was published in the *Écrits* with the title: "The mirror phase as formative of the I function as revealed in psychoanalytic experience."

In the 1930s, Lacan had already moved from Cartesian subject to Hegelian desiring subject. Then, after oscillating between Freud and Hegel, he elaborated the question of the desiring subject and formulated his own versions of subject and desire. According to Roudinesco, unlike contemporary psychologists, Lacan was more interested in the phenomenology of the mind. It is not, therefore, surprising that the IPA in 1936 was not interested in Lacan's work on the mirror phase; he had a more philosophical perspective regarding the image, ego formation and the other. It is important to distinguish the term "stage" from "phase". The mirror phase in Lacan's works in English has been wrongly translated as "mirror stage", reflecting a developmental aspect of the subject's mind rather than a structural phenomenon (Roudinesco, 2001). According to Lacan, as an effect of an encounter with his own image in the mirror, the individual is set off on the track of ego formation. This phase has a clear start and end in early childhood, which does not expand into the subject's adult life.

The 1949 version of the original paper is written more psychoanalytically. Furthermore, it focuses on the history of science. This reflects Lacan's own position as a psychoanalyst existing between differing schools of thoughts. More than philosophy this time, Lacan employed Freudian ideas beside linguistics and the theories of Claude Lévi-Strauss. These were pivotal elements in his 1949 version of the mirror phase paper.

A hole in the mirror

After 1949, from the specular image in the mirror and the body image, Lacan gradually moved toward theorising the Imaginary order as a part of the subject's structure. Regarding the body image, Lacan's position differs from that of Dolto. For Lacan, the fragmented body is seen and perceived as unified and coherent after the mirror phase. Dolto believes that the idea of a coherent body takes place even prior to this phase. For Lacan, the key object in this phase is the plane mirror. However, for Dolto, the symbolic object could be the voice and the eyes of the mother. In terms of the infant's reaction to his own body image, again Lacan's thesis indicates a sense of "jubilation" in the child, while Dolto suggests that such an encounter causes a sense of "suffering" and "symbolic castration" (Dolto, 1987).

When Lacan was still Freudian, his work concentrated on the narcissistic structure of the ego based on "me and my image". He never referred to the mirror phase as part of a mental developmental stage but rather as a phenomenon in which the ego (I) forms as a function. This coincides with Freud's theory on "primary narcissism" (Freud, 1914–1916). The advent of the ego, according to the earlier Lacan, happens through "primary narcissism". Around the same time, Klein had conceptualised the advent of the ego based on "primary object relations" (Klein, 1940).

In the 1950s, Lacan's ideas on the mirror phase move as follows: formation of (I) as a function resulting from alienation (méconnaissance) from the specular image → dual relations → Imaginary identification → the m(other)'s omnipotence causing a depressive reaction for the child and the formation of the "ego ideal" to eventually index the Symbolic order and the Other (Lacan, 1953–4, 1956–7).

The above trajectory leads us to understand Lacan's conceptualisation of the "subject". The subject is the most alienating phenomenon for an individual. All the descriptions one carries as a result of reality adaptation, cognitive perception, imagination and beliefs coincide with what is called "I", not a Lacanian subject. The significance of the mirror phase in Lacan's contribution to psychoanalysis can be understood as a revolutionary new perspective on the question of subjectivity. Up until then, Descartes – and later Hegel and Heidegger– viewed this question of subjectivity as including the philosophical version of "subject" in the realm of the Lacanian Imaginary register. In other words, the "subject" as a concept was limited to an illusion of "cogito".

In 1962, references to the mirror phase, the Symbolic order and the Other all appeared in Lacan's Seminar 10 (Lacan, 1962–3). The child is never alone with his specular image; the m(Other) speaks to the child about his image in the mirror. She names the image with the child's proper name, connecting the two by expressing her compliments. She adds description to the specular image of the child.

Although this reference to the m(O)ther's gaze is the advent of the concept of gaze (regard) in Lacan's teachings, it is not the first appearance of the symbolic gaze in the child's life; it just takes on another shape during the mirror phase. The gaze of the m(O)ther functions differently from the gaze of the image in the mirror for the child. The concept of gaze reappeared in Lacan's later work as the object of the scopic drive (Lacan, 1963–4).

Lacan's mirror phase became foundational to the theory of "subject" formation rather than merely being a theory of "I" or "ego" formation. From this perspective, autism and psychosis can also be understood. The failure of the Symbolic gaze, in the form of words of admiration or simply description, results in such conditions. In many clinical cases, when we explore the earliest experiences in the life of the infant with their caregiver, this failure manifests itself clearly. The caregiver's Symbolic position in this phase plays a fundamental role in making the child recognise himself not as a fragment of the mother but as an independent and whole entity. The absence of a sense of wholeness in the schizophrenic subject, or a radical refusal of the Symbolic in the autistic subject, are identified in detailed accounts of personal and familial histories. This goes beyond simply reducing the mirror phase to a psychical developmental stage in an infant's life or an identity formation.

This fundamental passage does not have to involve a real mirror and can take any metaphorical form. The start of the phase also can vary from one individual to another. Those who work with infants and very young children are familiar with this variation in starting time as well as in reactions. Discourse, which the child is born into, together with the caregiver's way of handling the child's needs and demands, creates the conditions within which the child will be introduced to the Symbolic order. The mOther's gaze has a subjective interpretation for each child. If this Symbolic gaze is too absent or too present, it leaves the child no Symbolic position from which to separate from the mOther.

A return ticket

After the child recognises his own specular image and gains a sense of mastery over it (Lacan, 1953–4), the identification with the image in the presence of the symbolic gaze leads the child to move from the "me" to the "I". Lacan gives the examples of the inverted bouquet and the vase in this context. The "I" is an individual waiting to become a subject. Although from the grammatical perspective, the passage from "me" to "I" indicated moving from an "object" to a "subject", the construction of a Lacanian subject involves a more complicated path, which includes all the three registers of Imaginary, Symbolic and Real in a specific arrangement in relation to desire and the drive.

The passage of *me to I*, the ego-formation, happens in both psychosis and neurosis. The function of the gaze in the mirror for a schizophrenic subject remains at a basic level maintaining the coherence of her/his body and mind. This function can be detected in many clinical cases of schizophrenia. The role of the mother/caregiver becomes minimalised to a literal function of the gaze in the mirror. It becomes a constant point of reassurance as well as of reference. In other words, it acts as a compass for a psychotic subject without which s/he cannot function in everyday life. Relating to the gaze remains in the Imaginary order. In one case, the patient's daily visit to his mother's place, even after her death, and recovering his everyday agenda in an informal report to the mother was one solution, making it possible for the patient to maintain the gaze. The short monologue to his mother every day allowed him to carry

out his other daily chores. He started his treatment after a change in his circumstances which prevented him from continuing this arrangement between
himself and the gaze. The question in this work was to substitute this basic yet
fundamental role of the gaze with another possible system. In this case, the
position of the analyst, handling the transference and the question of technique
and strategies, therefore, would revolve around the gaze function.

For a psychotic subject, a professional position in work or creation of artwork can play the same role as the gaze in the mirror. The theme of artwork
in a real case focusing on the presence of the gaze, had a sustainable role for
the patient in preserving the coherence of his body and mind as well as being
a point of reference for his existence.

Sometimes the subject puts himself in the position of the gaze looking
through it in order to reduce the intensity and intrusion of the mirror gaze.
This is another possible way in which to cope with the foreclosure of the Symbolic order.

The advent of the ego ideal, I(A) in Lacan's theory, is to be found in the
early 1950s (Lacan, 1953–4). The ego ideal, which anticipates the secondary
identification, is in fact an ideal signifier indexing the position of the subject in
the realm of the Symbolic order. Identifying with the Other's desire in neurotic
cases creates a scenario for each subject to embark on in life. The desire to be
or to become "such and such" in life has, in a neurotic subject, a more complicated arrangement than simply copying the ideals existing in the family discourse. In other words, a neurotic's relation with the gaze's function manifests
itself at the level of the subject of desire and drive. Lacan dedicated part of his
Seminar 11 to the concept of drive – as one of the four main concepts – of psychoanalysis. Drive is not the same as desire although there is a point of convergence
between the two. The gaze, which was elaborated as the object of the scopic drive
in Lacan's later teaching, does not remain merely at the level of the specular
image – Imaginary – or as a Symbolic function (Lacan, 1963–4).

The question of the body in the mirror that is the first Other experienced by the
subject prior to the Other of language differs radically in neurosis and psychosis.
The fragmented body in schizophrenia refers metaphorically to the lack of
a unifying coherence. The question of a unified and mastered body in Lacan's theories starts from the mirror phase and the specular image and leads to the speaking
body, the Real body. The Real body carries the invisible marks of Lalangue. The
effect of language at the level of the body concerns the way in which each body
enjoys. Furthermore, a broad range of symptoms and signs of which the subject
complains of as psychosomatic should not be reduced to biological factors or to
the relation of the subject to her/his body image (the Imaginary).

Therefore, in the Lacanian orientation, the role of the Symbolic mother as
the position of the gaze will move to the introducer of jouissance to the body.
The neurotic subject who complains of the speaking body will become able to
read the invisible lines of the Symbolic in the Real of the body through the
analysis of the semblances of language.

In analysis, changes in subjective position would be likely to occur once the patient becomes able to read the script of her/his fantasy of being/having/ becoming "such and such". However, the subject at the end of analysis arrives at an opaque and autistic point which is "the One"; unreadable, untranslatable and uninterpretable. This is a silence of the Real from which a subject had once escaped and entered into the Symbolic. The neurotic subject had decided to take a diversion from autism – the radical form of the Other's foreclosure – at a particular moment. This moment of departure requires a laborious examination and elaboration later in analysis, so as to be able to return to the mutism of the Real unconscious.

The position and function of narratives in the formation of the subject play a fundamental role. Although ultimately the subject of analysis arrives at a silent moment with a different position from where s/he had started their journey, a child's caregiver plays a symbolic role, rescuing him from the silence of the Real. The anguish is pacified and a topological position is given to the child through the medium of language. The mOther facilitates this introduction to the Symbolic through punctuating and handling the child's needs and demands. This function should not be reduced to either the constant background voice of a speaker or a silent and confusing communication. Overemphasis on either of these would create a confusing state for the child to submit only to the Imaginary of spoken language and meaning with a logic of cause and effect. The law of the Symbolic remains at the level of the Real and all the self-made constructions of the psychotic subject later in life would be an attempt to escape the overwhelming Real and find a way to deal with an earlier failure in the knot of being. They can be overwhelmed by bodily excitation or by meaning. Appreciating being alive or having a reason to continue living can be a major problematic for some psychotic patients. This self-creation, the synth-homme, is a term coined by Lacan in his analysis of the case of James Joyce in his Seminar 23 on sinthome (Lacan, 1975–6). There are different readings of the Joyce case in terms of his clinical diagnosis being a case of psychosis or perversion. Lacan had interpreted Joyce's style of writing as his sinthome. The sinthome in Joyce's case, according to Lacan, is the fourth ring which makes a psychotic subject's knot of being sustainable. In psychosis, the foreclosure of the Symbolic results in unravelling the knot. The sinthome as the fourth element in the Borromean knot can then make up for an earlier failure when there was not a symptom in place to rescue the child from an imposing law of the mother. In Lacan's reading of James Joyce, it was Joyce's unique style of writing which had prevented him from going mad. Furthermore, he had managed to make a name (fame) for himself through his work in literature. Therefore, he had formed an ego for himself. In other words, Joyce's sinthome and his ego are equated.

In this respect, the identity, originating from the mirror phase, in psychotic cases remains rather an abstract description of "what I am". The answer is a certain response to how close or far they seem to be from an ideal ego, i(a). A patient of mine recognises himself as a "bag of bones and blood". His artworks focus on depicting a cubism of his interior, which is distinguished from his exterior by a membrane of his dry skin. In neurosis, the subject anticipates to be or to have the phallus (as the signifier of a Symbolic lack), which involves an alienating process to form an unconscious strategy in relation to it, whereas for a psychotic subject the status of the phallus remains at the Imaginary level as an ideal image to copy, to follow or to identify with.

Hence, psychotic and neurotic subjects relate to the question of failure and success structurally in two different ways.

Le Silence de la Mèr(e)

In light of the mirror phase and the mOther's role in facilitating the child's path towards the Symbolic, the ideal ego and ego ideal's interplay in love, desire and narcissism, I would like to refer to a French novel by Vercors – Jean Bruller – written at the time of France's occupation in the early 1940s, *Le Silence de la Mer*.

From a forced encounter between two members of a French family and a German officer – Werner Von Ebrennac – a temporary occupier of their house, a resistance takes place. The German officer is a Francophile captain and a musician. In the eyes of his French hosts, he is nothing more than an enemy. Similar to any first encounter between two subjects, when there is no prior acquaintance between them and the relationship is restricted to the Imaginary register, the German officer is an enemy occupying France. The hosts decide to express their resistance through their silence. Every night, the officer salutes them and tries to share some words with them. However, all his attempts end up as nightly monologues. Through his brief but constant attempts, the family begins to know him and his background better. The captain's status gradually changes; his presence becomes more acceptable and tolerable. Increasingly he becomes anticipated by his hosts. Yet they do not break their resistance. The Francophile officer is patient and never fails to accommodate their rejections by his subtle interventions. He visits them with great care and in plain clothes rather than in Nazi uniform. In his monologues his position is well elaborated; he does not come across as an occupier. He is considerate and appreciative of their hospitality. A man emerges out of enemy uniform.

Now, the hosts have a *relationship* to him and his presence is accepted without acknowledging this through spoken words. In the absence of a conversation with him, they relate to him differently; beyond the Imaginary of the semblance, the Nazi uniform. The silence is still up in the air. The resistance and refusal to communicate via words still has a high symbolic value for the French hosts. The captain does not speak from a position of authority nor is he a constant talker. He is reassuring right from the beginning and gradually uses the language of culture beyond that of everyday life, chores and rituals. He becomes safe to listen to. He knows how to listen to their silence.

According to the early Lacan's schema of the two mirrors in the seminar of 31 March 1954, it can be inferred that the relationship between the two parties traverses the specular images of "this versus that". There is a mutual ideal between the two which is art: music and literature. Both sides relate to an ideal ego and ego ideal in the form of art and culture, a mutual "libidinal invested object". As a result of such "interplay" between ideal ego and ego ideal, a love and a desire arise. However, the concept of desire in the Lacanian orientation takes a turn into the Real and arrives at sexual non-rapport. Since each party in a love relation relates to her/his object of desire and takes jouissance from their own body independently, there is a desire on each side with sexual non-rapport. However, in this schema the position of the gaze is occupied by the subject and not the caregiver.

Werner's position in this novel can also be interpreted as the Symbolic mother striving to break the mutism and silence of the infant's resistance before submission to the Symbolic. His smart moves, knowing how to employ language, break the path of autism. He is not self-centred or impatient. He does not use the medium of language in a diverse and confusing way as could be the case with some multilingual mothers. He speaks and there are silent moments, thus giving a Symbolic position in the form of "respect" to the Other of his child/hosts. He anticipates their moves and allows them to take their time. His position gradually is separated from an omnipotent and omnipresent position.

In the French title of this novel, the term "mer" meaning sea has a homophony with the term "mère" meaning mother. We can also think of maternal jouissance as an engulfing sea from which a subject is supposed to escape by help of a symptom. In the Lacanian use of the Borromean knot, the symptom – as a translator of unconscious material to Real jouissance – is situated between the Symbolic and Real. What eventually separates a subject from an engulfing maternal jouissance is the symptom. Further to subjective signification of the equivocal mother tongue, the paternal metaphor finalises symptom formation. Lacan's emphasis on using the term "mother tongue" rather than, say, "mother's language" in his later teaching emphasised the Real of maternal jouissance rather than the Symbolic metaphor found in language. In other words, the tongue as a Real fleshy organ in the mouth was given more focus than the signifiers in spoken language (Lacan, 1975–6).

In Vercors' novel, once Werner's ideal in the Nazi philosophy of war collapses and he sees the nasty war from a different perspective, he decides to fade away. His fantasy had reached a limit and there seems to be no cause for which to fight. When he wants to leave, finally, the resistance of the silence breaks: "Please enter, Sir," the host says. He had spent night after night giving a structure to the relationship between himself and his hosts, anticipating these few words. The relationship between two parties, which was oscillating between the Real and the Imaginary, was eventually introduced to the third order, the Symbolic, with all its holes and misunderstandings as Antoine de Saint-Exupéry referred to in his Le Petit Prince. This short novel does not elaborate on that but ends at this moment, which was anticipated throughout the story.

The hosts also wanted, and chose, to get engaged in the relationship with the captain. Finally, the silence of the hostess breaks with a last, single word: "Adieu."

Conclusion

In Lacan's theories of the mirror phase, one can observe his trajectory from rejecting the biological perspective in understanding the child's encounter with his specular image to the phenomenology of the Imaginary. From the phenomenology of the specular image and the physics of the object and the mirror, he moves to the topology of subject's position. Finally, Lacan begins formulating the concept of the subject beyond the philosophical Cartesian subject, beyond the Imaginary and Symbolic to arrive at a Real topological position of the subject.

Although the mirror phase is the first major contribution of Lacan to psychoanalysis, it became a starting point from which his later theories of the subject, desire and drive were elaborated on. As we saw earlier, in the English translation of the mirror phase from "Le Stade du Miroir" in French, some have used the term "stage" which does not reflect the true meaning of the concept. This phase, acting as a foundation for forming the ego and later the subject, is not a psychological developmental stage. Furthermore, the mirror phase should not be understood as the only and final way of explaining the formation of the subject but rather as its very foundation.

Bibliography

Borch-Jacobsen, M. (1990). *Lacan: The Absolute Master*. Stanford: Stanford University Press.

Dolto, F. (1987). *L'enfant du miroir*. Paris: Payot, 2002.

Freud, S. (1914–1916). On Narcissism. In: J. Strachey, ed., *The Standard Edition of the Complete Psychological Works of Sigmund Freud, Vol* XIV, pp. 67–107. London: Vintage, 2001.

Klein, M. (1940). Mourning and its relation to manic depressive states. *The International Journal of Psychoanalysis*, 21: 1940, 25–153.

Lacan, J. (1953–4). *The Seminar of Jacque Lacan: Book1: Freud's Paper on Technique*. John Forrester (Trans). New York & London: Norton.

Lacan, J. (1956–7). *Le séminaire de Jacques Lacan. Book IV: La relation d'objet*. Paris: Seuil, 1994.

Lacan, J. (1962–3). *The Seminar of Jacque Lacan: Book X: Anxiety*. A.R Price (Trans). Cambridge: Polity.

Lacan, J. (1963–4). *The seminar of Jacque Lacan: Book XI: Four Fundamental Concepts of Psychoanalysis*. Alan Sheridan (Trans). New York & London: Norton.

Lacan, J. (1966a). *Écrits: Subversion Du Sujet Et Dialectique Du Désir, 1960*, pp. 793–827. Paris: Seuil.

Lacan, J. (1966b). *Écrits: The Mirror stage as Formative of the I Function as Revealed in Psychoanalytic Experience, 1949*, pp. 75–82. Bruce Fink (Trans). New York & London: Norton.

Lacan, J. (1975–6). *Le Séminaire Livre XXIII : Le Sinthome*. Paris: Seuil.

Roudinesco, E. (2001). *L'analyse, L'archive*. Paris: Éditions de la Bibliothèque nationale de France.

Vercors. (2001). *Le Silence de la mer*. Paris: Magnard.

Wallon, H. (1983). *Les Origines du caractère chez l'enfant. Les préludes du sentiment de personnalité*. Paris: PUF.

Zazzo, R. (1948). *Reflets de miroir et autres doubles*. Paris: PUF, 1992.

Chapter 3

Memento

"I have this condition ..."

Psychosis and the past

The time of the unconscious

"I have this condition," he explained. "It's not amnesia. I have no short-term memory. I know who I am. I know myself well."

Since "his injuries", he had been unable to make new memories; in medical terms, this condition is known as *anterograde amnesia*. He could not remember what he had said or done in the past few minutes. He could not recall what had been registered by his brain. Nothing new of his daily interactions appeared to stick in his mind. From one moment to the next, he was living in the present, while hoping for a future in which he would be able to accomplish his mission of revenge. This was his purpose in life: a wish for vengeance. His last recorded memory was that of his wife's death, and he wanted to find her attacker and kill him. Driven by his goal of revenge, he had found ways to tackle his amnesiac condition. He had created a system of physical tools and reminders for himself, which he could refer to every time he found himself confused as to what was happening around him, in relation to other people. He carried photographs with some lines of description on them in his pocket, and words tattooed on his body acted as agents instructing him towards a course of action.

Jonathan and Christopher Nolan made the movie summarised above in 2000, inventing a new style of narrating a single plot while playing with the concept of chronological time. The movie follows two alternate chronologies, giving two ways of recounting the series of events: one travelling forward and the other going backwards in time. From these two narratives, the viewer slowly pieces together the jigsaw puzzle of the plot. At a certain point of the movie, at which these two times meet, the viewer supposes that s/he has grasped the plot. However, precisely at this point of convergence comes the twist, as a third line of events appears and we find we have been misled by the whole narrated plot up until this moment. This is when we might ask: was the protagonist really suffering from his amnesiac condition?

One might even have to re-watch this movie several times to understand how the plot is constructed. In addition to the objective and subjective narratives of the series of events, which are depicted in colour and black-and-white scenes respectively – showing the lure of the Imaginary register – we are able to observe the agency of a psychotic subject in manipulating truth and facts to create a new version of himself – synth-homme – (Lacan, 1975–6) after a triggered psychosis. A highly stable psychotic structure having been triggered at a certain point meant a psychotic episode followed by the recreation of a new mode of living. Such a mode gave specific meaning to the subject's being in relation to the Other.

The Nolan brothers' movie *Memento* also exemplifies one way in which to understand the concept of logical time in Lacan's teaching. In a paper of 1945, *Logical Time and the Assertion of Anticipated Certainty*, he refers to the dialectical structure of time and temporality, which in fact contradicts the familiar idea of time moving along a continuum (Lacan, 1953–4). In *Memento*, the recollection of past events as they appear to have happened to the subject in the present moment is all one narrative, the *après coup* in Lacanian terms; while the actual reality of past events is depicted in a second narrative, and shown to be different. However, the third way of making sense of events – only brought in as a narrative later on in the movie – shows how the realisation of truth momentarily shatters Leonard's imagined anticipated revenge, which gave him purpose to live his life. When this climactic moment arrives, the subject chooses to manipulate and falsify the truth in order to create a mode of living in that precise moment of hesitation: a moment to conclude. In an a-temporal structure of time, a historical event, subjectively recollected, along with his anticipation of an action to take – a hope – concludes an urgency to make a decision at a very precise moment in the present.

In this chapter, we will approach the question of self-creation in a psychotic subject in relation to the remembering and forgetting of past history.

Synth-homme

For a psychotic subject, not being able to remember the past can sometimes be as unsettling as remembering it clearly and constantly. In other words, there is a specific function to how and how much of a past is remembered or forgotten, by a psychotic subject. A remembered past could act as a point of reference. In the movie *Memento*, the male protagonist, Leonard Shelby, subjectifies his past and chooses to remember it only in a certain way. His condition of so-called amnesia, affecting his short-term memory, means that he desperately clings on to his tools and strategies in order to keep a grip on the facts he himself had created. *Memento* is a great way to understand the constant dilemma of a psychotic subject, who relentlessly invents and employs a construction to compensate for the failure of the paternal metaphor in the Symbolic order to have taken place much earlier in life.

To negativise the excessive jouissance that brings tension to his mind and body, Leonard creates meaning for his own life. He invents and masters a system made up of his Polaroids and tattoos. They are, in fact, his points of reference, rather than actually being reminders of what is forgotten. He cannot remember any encounter with the Other. In truth, his only real "memento" is the memory of a traumatic scene, that of his wife's death, which occurred a few years prior to the present time of the movie. He had devised and formed a solution – seeking revenge – which was now his guiding compass in life. He had watched his wife raped and assaulted when he himself was unable to move after a blow to the head. His psychic life after witnessing this scene, as well as the loss of his wife (who, it turns out, had been lethally over-medicated by Leonard himself), underwent a complete change.

One could also interpret this particular psychotic trigger through a Freudian lens: Leonard has witnessed a Freudian primal scene, such as Freud referred to in the Wolfman case (Freud, 1917–1919). Freud's interpretation, however, does not exactly reflect our means of understanding the cause of Leonard's psychotic episode and later his battle against his new condition of amnesia. What seemed to be the challenge to Leonard's stability in this case is that the violent crime scene had confronted him with the question of paternity and unsettled his role as protector; a classical interpretation of a father figure. Indeed, wasn't it an act of over-protecting when Leonard compulsively injected insulin into his diabetic wife, causing her death?

What about his life after he eventually managed to get his revenge on the rapist? Well, towards the end of the movie, Teddy, the undercover police officer who had apparently believed in Leonard's condition and supported him, revealed to Leonard that he had actually found and killed his wife's rapist a year previously. Since then, however, Leonard had continued playing the murderous game he had invented for himself, over and over, every time creating a better story behind his wife's assault, inspired by another man's life called Sammy Jankis. Leonard knew of this con man before his psychosis was triggered. Sammy did not have a wife in real life and Leonard had exposed his fraud from the insurance company which Leonard was working for at the time. However, Leonard had changed Sammy's story in the way he wanted it to be applied to his own condition. He had projected the death of his own wife onto Sammy's story. That is why Teddy believed that Leonard was not a natural-born killer but was, rather, skilled at creating endless games: "… that's why you are so good at it." In other words, such conditioning had not only lessened Leonard's guilt over the death of his wife, it had created a system of endless games.

Through the lens of psychoanalysis, the repetitions in Leonard's games and ever-changing stories are not simply a conversion or telling lies to oneself; they are part of a self-made system working to avoid any intrusion from the Real. Leonard seemed to be a family man, working hard in an insurance company, providing for his wife. At the point at which he encountered his trigger, he was confronted with an earlier failure of the Symbolic register. At that point, his well-suited position as provider/protector of the other (his wife) failed. We are not given many details of his past, as a child growing up, in order to learn more about why such a position had functioned well for him up until that moment. All we know is that, from the moment his psychosis was triggered, the way he lived his life changed dramatically, as if he was dethroned from that particular position. Indeed, this is like many psychotic male patients whose sexuality would be reduced to the question of being or not being emasculated by another rival in winning over a love interest.

No pathology found

Did he really want to get rid of his *anterograde amnesia*? This would be, perhaps, a better wording for the question we asked earlier, regarding his actual suffering from this condition. While his condition seems a real nuisance from an outside perspective, it has in fact done him a favour. Leonard was able to deal with the problem of the Other (of body and of language) after his trauma by manipulating his medical condition. He did not invent his amnesia – as a manifestation of his psychosis, for example – he was only manipulating the facts of his situation in order to pin down a single, suitable meaning out of the chaos in his mind.

In contrast to how he seemed up until a certain point in the movie – a victim, or, perhaps, a hero seeking justice for his wife's death – he was shown to not be as innocent as he had previously appeared. He was not a victim; in fact, the position of victim was exactly that symbolic position which did *not* suit him at all. All his tools and strategies were efforts to avoid being placed in such a position. Leonard had used his amnesiac condition as an ally, which created meanings for him that tackled any unwanted invasion of the Real. The practice of tattooing was also another functional way to deal with the unlocalised libido in his body. All others out in the world were divided into two: either friends or enemies, reflecting a psychotic solution to the enigmatic desire of the Other. He believed only what he wanted to believe; that the alluring Imaginary was agent in all the choices he made was only revealed later in the movie.

This challenges the medical explanation, if there is any solid one, about the relationship between head trauma and certain patients' conditions, such as amnesia, depersonalisation, impaired ability to employ language, etc. Physical harm in addition to neurological defects will definitely have physio-psychological effects – as it changes the functions of the body – but there is always a symbolic dimension to such traumas. The way in which a neurotic subject takes up a position in response to bodily changes can radically differ from a psychotic subject's position; it is the underlying question that is raised for the subject that differentiates the two structures of the psyche. The neurotic and the psychotic subjects might even initially respond similarly, at a cognitive level, but in the longer-term we see how the effects of trauma are dealt with differently. With a severe or traumatic injury, there is almost always the need to remember the details of what happened before and afterwards. So, in both structures, there is an active agency that works upon a certain encounter and deals with the aftermath.

As opposed to the objective interpretation of the cause of psychosis in medicine with regards to the patient's past history, in psychoanalysis the question of the subject's past, their personal history and their relationship to chronological time is considered subjectively. The way in which a certain memory in the past is given subjective significance can tell us what orients a psychotic patient in relation to the Other. Moreover, the function of forgetting the past, or, conversely, attempting to remember it, is one way to understand the differential diagnosis in psychosis besides the subject's relation to the problematic of meaning, libido and the Other (Leader, 2011). The psychotic structure would range from the narcissistic imprisonment of a schizophrenic subject to the Other's gaze, to a melancholic's exhaustive self-blame in relation to the Other; from the Other's conspiracies around the subject's destiny in paranoia, to a manic-depressive's personal mission of doing good in the world (Leader, 2013). Of course, not all patients with the same structural diagnosis share the same sets of symptoms and signs; many clinicians who work with psychosis can find it sometimes challenging to make a differential diagnosis between the four categories of psychosis, from a structural point of view. However, the type of clinical approach to the direction of treatment will not matter, as long as the clinician's work is oriented towards a psychotic structure.

The black mirror

In *Memento*, the film-makers' aim was to show that the facts we base our lives around are not always true. Moreover, the Nolan brothers tend to explain the difference between objective and subjective narratives of a single event in terms of how a subject is able to deceive himself through the use of certain images. However, Nolan's interpretation of subjective truth might not reflect exactly what we refer to in the concept of subjectivity. Lacan's theory of the *mirror phase* is considered to be the foundation of subject formation (Lacan, 1953–4). This theory was discussed in the previous chapter. A subject has the agency to choose whether or not to believe, reject or manipulate a truth.

In clinical treatment, a psychotic patient could have serious difficulties around remembering a traumatic past, and it would be crucial to explore whether the patient's struggle lies with finding a way to recall and express his memories so that, for example, he could change his relation to that specific trauma and move on with his life, or, whether he was adhering to his amnesia as a way of filling the gaps of the Real. In *Memento*, for example, Leonard did not contract a disorder after a head injury causing an amnesia; he avoided the Real of the trauma of what he had witnessed. The traumatic scene had brought him face-to-face with a hole in the mirror, situating the gaze in that hole, confronting him. This recent event brought up what was already foreclosed for him, in the Symbolic realm of early life. The movie states that his condition is that he cannot make any new memories since the trauma. However, his inability to make any new memories – as a psychotic phenomenon – is as a result of his refusal to submit to the Symbolic order rather than to the recent trauma. Instead, he is constantly inventing new versions of reality for both himself and the others around him. It is not clear at what point his self-invented system will fail him. Will this system with which he finds a way around his psychical inability to access the Symbolic be crushed when he ultimately kills Teddy, who had made use of Leonard for his own ends, but had also protected him from the State's law? As the movie does not show us the aftermath, we will never know. However, we can imagine, from Leonard's incredible ability to transform a disaster into a new way of life, that he will continue to construct increasingly better versions of a system suiting his condition. What could possibly go wrong for such a brilliant engineer of meaning?

The domain of language offers many opportunities and possible functions to a human being. If a neurotic is well-suited to employ the complicated, multiple layers of language, a psychotic limits himself to meanings in the simpler domain of language. This does not mean a psychotic is unable to make jokes or play with aspects of language in order to convey humour or horror to the outside world. Nor does it mean that there is no structure as such in their daily life. The Symbolic order, however, is associated with a hole or lack; a *méconnaissance* and discontinuity. What distinguishes a psychotic from a neurotic position here is the structural relation to the symbolic law of language. Natalie, the female protagonist in *Memento*, was also using Leonard's condition to fight her battle against Teddy. Both Natalie's and Teddy's characters, as portrayed in this movie, seem to show a different subjective position towards the Other's desire to that which Leonard takes. As Lacan said, a psychotic subject is inhabited, possessed by language (Lacan, 1955–6). His effort to leave or avoid the void of the Real brings the practice of exorcism to mind. Such a process can become problematic, even impossible – hopefully, momentarily – for some psychotic patients, when they cannot access their short-term or long-term memory after the trigger of their illness – but this is not the same as forgetting who they are.

Psychoanalysis and the clinic

The intention behind wanting to remember, in whatever way a subject might want to remember, differs from case to case. In one clinical example, the patient wanted to remember what her childhood was like in order to learn about "the taste of life", as she had forgotten a "carefree" way to live in the present. Questioned around the meaning of "carefree", it turned out that she meant literally "free of care": "No tags on." At that time, her daily life was strictly controlled by her father after she had come out of rehab. Her wish to access memories stemmed from finding her own solutions and to learn from the past, to deal with her addiction to drugs and self-cutting.

A while ago, a patient visited me searching for an explanation of her childhood fainting episodes that had been followed by amnesia. She was able to remember the context of her fainting, but wanted to restore her incomplete memories of the details during and after her episodes. Initially, she wanted a prescription – as the quickest shortcut to solve her problem – but fear of the medication's possible side-effect of further amnesia put her off. However, such initial urgency to resolve her issue showed how much she was distressed by her loss of certain memories of the past. This was a case of melancholia in which the subject did not seem to be bothered by "meaning in flux", as is the case with schizophrenia. She was a devoted mother to her children and this was what had helped her to keep going, until she learned that her son was a drug addict. She then remembered that her own uncle had died suddenly due to a long-term addiction to heroin when she was a child. Her main question in the clinical work was certainly not explicitly about her own suffering – severe agitation and anxiety – but, rather, how to help her son to survive his condition. She reproached herself for not being a "responsible mother" for her son. Her care for the others around her was what steered her life choices and what she needed to restore from her past – the events in her childhood around her uncle's life and death – was a way to understand what she did wrong in her own son's upbringing. She could not remember the events of her childhood in her adult life and did not seem to be bothered by this until her highly stable psychosis was triggered. Her fainting and the episodes of amnesia took place around the time of her much-loved uncle's death from an overdose.

In many cases of melancholia, the subject does not end up in a consulting room voluntarily unless their own self-reproach becomes unbearable or causes discomfort to others around them: a partner or a child, a friend or a colleague, might be affected by the patient's course of action. The majority of the work would usually be around this other's circumstances, which are supposed to be caused by the melancholic subject her- or himself. In terms of their past and history, the melancholic subject is highly likely to circle around a single event to which they assign sole responsibility for changing their relationship to this other in their family or community. The destructive jouissance of self-blame could be transformed into active efforts towards making up for what they have supposedly done wrong in relation to the Other. As opposed to the schizophrenic subject, such as the one we referred to earlier, for a melancholic subject, it is highly uncommon to forget past events. What is remembered and how it is remembered both have a particular meaning, and point the finger of blame towards them.

For a paranoiac subject, a single event in the past can be given significance and meaning linked to an Other that is responsible for the subject's miseries. A very quiet and punctual paranoiac subject who had a successful long-term career had for several weeks been utterly unable to leave his home after the sudden discovery, by accident, of his father's historical unfaithfulness. His mother had remained silent about the incident for personal reasons. He blamed them both; not only for dismissing the event between themselves but also for hiding it from him. "What else have they hidden from me?" he asked himself, over and over again. This was a truly unsettling question for him. After a period of serious depression, followed by constant, tormenting thoughts about his relationship with his parents, he decided to seek a talking cure. In the first meeting, his main requirement from therapy seemed to be an investigation of his personal history, which would gather up all pieces of information and documentation about his family's past so that he would eventually be able to rewrite the history of his childhood based on objective findings. In other words, it seemed that he wanted to make a sort of documentary of his past. Similar to Leonard in *Memento*, who had created a system to avenge his wife's assault, he was acting to restore justice, acting as prosecution and judge, and was only seeking a talking cure as a third-party witness. His basic belief in the morality of truth over lies had been shaken. What seemed important in his case was not only the emphasis he laid on finding out a single truth, but also that he wanted to document and record his past as evidence. The Other was pointing at him, which was causing him a great deal of mental torture. However, as is expected within the treatment of paranoia, he was exercising his destructive mode of jouissance through documentation to an excessive extent. It was the Other – his parents and their "life full of lies" – that needed to be sanitised and brought to judgment. He would have made a good documentary film-maker!

Past time for a paranoiac subject has a repetitive, circular movement rather than the broken record it might be for a schizophrenic. For this reason, amnesia about the past within the paranoiac structure is, again, very uncommon, particularly due to the fact that documentation and paying a great deal of attention to detail is given so much emphasis within this structure. The relation of a paranoiac subject to past events is solid in terms of the possibility of change. If Leonard was able to give the past many different subjective interpretations, a paranoiac subject places emphasis on what was perceived by him at the time, and interprets it as solid fact. Working with a paranoiac subject can be difficult for precisely this reason. Blaming past events gives the subject an anchoring point, which helps them to live with certain difficulties in their current life in relation to the Other. As meaning is fixed in paranoia – it's always the Other's fault – the possibility of modifying this kind of relationship could come about through an exploration of the cause(s) of the past events. In both paranoia and melancholia, it takes much longer than in schizophrenia and manic-depression to help the subject construct and modify his relationship with a personal history.

In psychoanalysis, it is crucial to examine the different functions that forgetting and remembering the past can have in different cases. In some cases of psychosis, an uneventful past operates as a pacifier for the subject, while in other cases this is unsettling. As well as the obviously long-forgotten events of early childhood, there might be some gaps in a subject's memory dating from more recent years, as was the case with Leonard. Finding out the answer to "what happened?" at those times could offer a psychotic subject a new meaning, filling a gap in the Real and, beyond that, even making for a turning point in a psychotic episode. A shift in the subject's position can potentially give a new direction in life and rescue him from being overwhelmed by a state of a jouissance.

In many ways, manic-depressive psychosis can be confused with schizophrenia, or vice versa. The common feature between the two is the rapidity with which changes occur after the trigger. The main changes of clinical interest are to do with creativity. This creativity could be a solution to make up for the failure of the paternal metaphor, particularly after experiencing an episode of psychosis as a rather common manifestation in many cases (Leader, 2011). However, while a manic-depressive subject uses his creativity as a force to effect as large a change in the outside world as possible, a schizophrenic subject strives to find a safe space in his creative practice, from which he can interact with others.

In both schizophrenia and manic-depression, the past in recent or distant memory is easily forgotten or dismissed for various reasons. Exploring a certain event or series of events in the past can easily bore a manic-depressive, while being difficult to go back to for a schizophrenic – as the past represents something out of their control and exploring it can bring out new, unsettling meanings for their present.

In manic-depression, we usually find the subject focused on a future that promises excitement ahead. This makes it difficult to reconstruct a past history for them but this work of reconstruction can slow down their mind's processing speed, which is in fact a mode of jouissance for the subject. Hence, it is crucial to introduce temporal metrics to limit the excess of overexcitement, which is indeed disturbing. The past is only referred to voluntarily if it is a source of pride for some manic-depressive subjects. From this, they can derive a sense of safety. By focusing on the element of continuity in time, they can potentially calm down and feel settled for a while. In both schizophrenia and manic-depression, the past is broken into a series of significant events. It would be important in clinical treatment to elaborate on what, exactly, has made these historical events important to the subject, before intervening around them in any way.

Another question which can be raised regarding psychosis and the perception of time is the time of year at which the triggering of a psychotic phenomenon or episode occurs. At a specific time of the year – say, a significant anniversary – a psychotic subject might start to feel unsettled. The first question is to uncover what sort of question or enigma the subject is faced with, that leads them to reach out for help. There are many cases of psychosis in which the subject is well aware that at a particular time of the year they need a professional intervention, which could range from medication or hospitalisation to therapy or a talking cure. For the clinician, a psychotic patient is often the best teacher in terms of how to find help. Here, the patient is master in finding new ways to tackle the issue of a destructive jouissance. For example, a manic-depressive case taught me a while ago not to fail to encourage him to go as far as he could go – in the geographical sense – when springtime approached. This particular time of the year coincided with the anniversary of his father's death, several years before. He had "a special relationship" with his father, as he was "his rescuer" from a very strict mother. After seeing his father pass away, the subject experienced overwhelming feelings of excitement all over his body, which was followed by compulsive vomiting. He remembered then running as fast as he could – he could not remember for how long – until he collapsed in the street: this was his first experience of a psychotic episode. He did not have any memory of running, how far and why so fast, or any idea why he had done it, but apparently it had helped him reset his system against the rush of excessive sensation throughout his body.

A schizophrenic subject called me up one day, asking for a consultation about a recent episode he had experienced, which involved being unable to remember how he had ended up in Accident & Emergency after a gathering at his friend's home. This temporary amnesia was causing him a great deal of anguish. He was not even able to focus his attention on our conversation, and was extremely agitated. At A&E, he had been prescribed a tranquiliser and some sleeping pills, but this had made his condition much worse, as he desperately wanted to recollect his recent memory in order to conquer the anxiety about what he had done during the amnesia. Putting him to sleep was not a stroke of genius on that particular occasion! After the initial episode, he had begun getting horrifying visual hallucinations. To deal with these, he found a temporary solution by becoming a visual artist: he found a way to make sense of the content of his hallucinations in work and transformed a sort of a non-sense in his illustrations and drawings, establishing a meaning in his mind. However, after a short while his creation of artworks became overwhelming. The content of the artworks, at this point, were repetitive patterns, usually in geometrical shapes. After further investigation of his new condition, as well as his family history, it turned out that his father was a geometer, and he could not bear any allusion to his (real) father. It did not take him long – fortunately – to come up with another solution to find some sense in the void of the Real. He now became interested in using some of the traumatic events of his life as material for satirical sketches. The humour transformed the Real of the trauma into a creative work, while bringing him recognition from the gaze of his family members and close friends, which was exactly suited to solve his problems. The familiar gaze, in this case, gave his existence some coherence. He never published his works.

Psychosis and contemporary society

In recent years, there is a growing popular interest in finding out about one's ancestry. One psychotic subject's way of dealing with what had been foreclosed for him was to trace back a past which was not simply forgotten but actually lost. He benefited from the development of DNA tracing. In this clinical case, the subject's father was not known to him, and he used to blame all his miseries in life on this fact. He was not able to remember much of his childhood. This particular amnesia became unsettling for him at the age of 25 when his girlfriend pushed him to share some events of his childhood with her. His self-diagnosis was *retrograde amnesia*. His explanation of this condition was that his memories had been wiped clean from his brain due to a heavy ingestion of ecstasy during his teenage years. He eventually decided to set himself the impossible task of tracing his genetic code back many thousands of years. He was actually successful in this mission impossible, and re-wrote a personal history in the form of an imaginary autofiction. Although in this case there was not any automatic or active mode of remembering or forgetting the past, he had found a sort of knowledge which gave meaning to who he was; as a son of his "ancestors" rather than the son of an unknown dad.

If, for a neurotic subject, an email or a text reminder, or even an old-fashioned post-it, is simply a way to help him recollect data regarding an event, for some psychotic subjects, in cases similar to Leonard's, such elements are ways of getting them to interact in their daily life. For these subjects, it is not simply a matter of these being easy to use or being anything to do with our increasing reliance on technical devices; it is that they do not have any recollection of the past events. In *Memento*, Leonard was not lying about his desire to avenge his wife; he had found a rather twisted way to carry on living with it. A schizophrenic patient was not able to remember appointments or arrangements without any third-party intervention – such as his PA – reminding him, every day, several times a day, of his errands. He could not register any words or conversation that involved temporal arrangements. His solutions, from mobile phone reminders to his emails and ultimately to employment of a PA, had tempered the chaos of his everyday life to a certain extent. However, he wanted to understand why he had this condition. Through clinical work, it became clear that the situations he had amnesia around were those that involved, for him, the need to explain himself. In this case of psychosis, the question, "who am I for the Other?" put him under the spotlight of a Symbolic gaze, something that he did not know how to deal with. He even referred to himself using his first name rather than the pronoun "I".

Conclusion

For a human being, having a subjective history to either remember or refer to, or even get amnesia about, is necessary – regardless of any questions about the structure of the psyche. Yet this takes on a rather different meaning in psychosis in terms of the subject's relation to the Other of language. Likewise, for a psychotic subject, the issue of being remembered can differ from case to case, ranging from being remembered for a mission in life to something to avoid completely.

For Leonard in *Memento*, neither his tattoos nor his Polaroids were actual reminders; they were just hints giving him new instructions for each day. The variations of the names "John G." on his notes and "Sammy Jankis" tattooed on his hand, were names to work through anew every time he rediscovered them. They carried with them no specific meaning or any reminder of a particular past experience. He invented a different reason behind each of them, every single time. They were certainly not reminders or mementos; they acted more like pins, to suture the gap in signification, the *points de capiton*, (Lacan, 1955) which somewhat stabilised his condition. From this perspective, *Memento* is a deceptive title for this great movie, unless the subjective memory of an image from the recent past, that of Leonard's wife dying, is what is being referred to here.

Bibliography

Freud, S. (1917–1919). From the history of an infantile neurosis. In: J. Strachey, ed., *The Standard Edition of the Complete Psychological Works of Sigmund Freud, Vol XVII*, pp. 1–122. London: Vintage, 2001.

Lacan, J. (1953–4). *The Seminar of Jacque Lacan: Book I: Freud's Paper on Technique*. John Forrester (Trans). New York & London: Norton.

Lacan, J. (1955–6). *The Seminar of Jacques Lacan: Book III: The Psychoses*. J.-A. Miller (ed), (Trans) Russell Grigg. London: Routledge, 1993.

Lacan, J. (1966). *Écrits: Logical Time and the Assertion of Anticipated Certainty*. pp. 196–197. Bruce Fink (Trans). New York & London: Norton.

Lacan, J. (1975–6). *Le Séminaire Livre XXIII: Le Sinthome*. Paris: Seuil.

Leader, D. (2011). *What is Madness?* London: Hamish Hamilton.

Leader, D. (2013). *Strictly Bipolar*. London: Penguin.

Chapter 4

Inside out?

Symptom formation

Introduction

About two decades ago we were on our morning rounds in the surgery ward of a training hospital, discussing the case of a patient with fever and severe abdominal pains. We were meant to be making a list of potential diagnoses based on his symptoms and signs. The general surgeon of the ward wanted to make a decision about whether or not to go in with a McBurney's Incision, for an open appendectomy. He emphasised the importance of symptoms in patients as signs of underlying issues. A set of symptoms signals a disease or a disorder from which one concludes a meaning: the clinical diagnosis. In the absence of symptoms, however, an unlucky patient would end up without a cure. A diagnosis also considers how poor or fair the prognosis of an illness is. For instance, with a Krukenberg ovarian tumour or in the case of oesophageal cancer, once symptoms manifest, the patient would have only a few weeks or months left to live. In other words, in medicine we cannot have a diagnosis without a symptom as its manifestation. The patient suffers from it and is certain that treating the symptom will set her free. Therefore, treating and hopefully getting rid of it orient the direction of treatment. On the other hand, the cause and origin of symptom formation, from a medical perspective, could range from being an idiopathic to a pathological change, to the physiology of a "biological" body.

In 2015, Pixar–Disney released *Inside Out,* an animated film focusing on a human's emotions as they affect her relationship with others. The emphasis on the so-called neuro-psychological function of the brain as what was responsible for a subject's course of actions and mode of decision-making was a simplistic way to think, in terms of a human subject with a Real body. One cannot deny the effects of neurotransmitters and hormones on the functions of the body. However, such a view reduces – if not completely denies – a human subject's evolution into a being that has become able to carry out relatively complicated tasks by relying on a more complex brain function compared to other animals. It is indeed saddening to learn that new generations are led to conceive of a human subject's relation to others only through cognitive science. As the result of such a view, too much emphasis is put on personality and presentation rather than on the agency of the subject who owns a very complicated body, and enjoys it.

On a separate note, each of the Pixar–Disney animated characters in *Inside Out*, who are given the names of affects, could be considered as a representative of the different psychical structures in psychoanalysis: Sadness (melancholic psychosis), Joy (manic-depressive psychosis), Disgust (hysteria), Fear (obsessional neurosis) and Anger (schizophrenia).

Freudian discovery

In the *Neuro-Psychoses of Defence*, Freud conceptualises the symptom as a substitute for sexual ideas incompatible with the reality of the subject's life. He also refers to the shape or surface of the symptom as changing from one person to the next. Most of the examples in this article, however, are from obsession and phobia in psychosis (Freud, 1893–1899). Despite being a medical doctor, Freud himself initially noticed something about the clinical symptoms discussed in *Conversion Hysteria* as early as the late nineteenth century, as shown in his letters to Fliess. According to Freud, a symptom was a way to fulfil a wish arising from a repressed thought. He gives us the example of a hysterical woman who was suffering from vomiting, without any organic cause. Freud interpreted her symptom as a wish for pregnancy. In another example, he refers to a case named "Mr E.", who turned red and sweaty in encounters with others. Freud's explanation concerned the patient's repressed thoughts about being the "deflowerer" of the person in question (Freud, 1886–1899).

Much later, in 1916, the symptom was considered as the substitute for a frustration. Such a substitute is created as a result of the libido regressing to an earlier time of object choice. Symptom formation starts as early as the age of 4 or 5 and has a repressed infantile sexuality as its main motivating force. Freud puts the Oedipus complex at the core of symptom formation as well as being the cause of neurosis. According to him, the ego's defence mechanism results in symptom formation. Moreover, at this stage in Freud's work, symptom – as a substitute – has a sexual motive, which finds means of expression after the ego fails to keep it repressed (Freud, 1916–1917).

Later, in 1926, in his *Inhibitions, Symptoms and Anxiety*, Freud states that the symptom is not a part of the ego but rather an ego function, and links symptom formation to castration anxiety and separation anxiety, both of which involve loss of the object. Elaborating on the element of compulsion in obsessional neurosis, he associates it with an obsessive's fixation on the "anal phase", as the result of regression. Here, Freud distinguishes hysteria and obsessional neurosis based on their mechanism of symptom formation. He blames symptom formation in the former on repression only, while the latter is the result of ego defences such as regression, reaction formation, etc. In neurosis, the symptom is the result of repression formed in order to avoid anxiety. He also admits that the subject's ego searches for some satisfaction through the symptom (Freud, 1925–6). After all, it is the substitute for making a sacrifice!

Freud's reading of Little Hans' phobia of horses was that it was a substitute/ symptom for his fear of his father (Freud, 1909), while the Wolfman's homosexual desire was displaced with a phobia of wolves (Freud, 1917–1919). In the same fashion, Schreber's persecutory delusion – being his symptom – was formed as a result of the ego's defence mechanism: projection (Freud, 1911–1913). In terms of the symptomology of psychotics, Freud's elaboration focuses on the ego's function in terms of how far it can resist in this battle. If it loses its strength, psychosis is triggered (Freud, 1924).

The above sketch of Freud's work on symptom formation is focused on the ego's function. Furthermore, Freud had distinguished the symptom, as an unconscious formation, from slips of the tongue, jokes and bungled actions. His attention to the very existence of such formations revolutionised medical views, particularly in the clinic of *hysteria*. Although Lacan formed a different conceptualisation of symptom formation after Freud, certain elements of the symptom remained the same, such as repetition and compulsion, the symptom being an unconscious (as in, non-organic and non-cognitive) formation, signalling a discomfort in the psyche and its relation to the drive.

Symptom/sinthome

Unlike in medicine, which uses the term "symptom" as the sign of a so-called "disorder", in psychoanalysis a symptom is perceived as a "repair" in itself. In neurosis, a subject's division is somewhat repaired through symptom formation. The term is used in the neurotic structure rather than in psychosis and perversion (Lacan, 1958b). As there is not a general description for all subjects' symptom patterns and functions, the process through which a symptom is formed is not a process that is common for all neurotics. Lacan's discussion of how and why a symptom is formed contradicts the Freudian idea of such an unconscious formation. However, he still agreed with Freud on the fact that the symptom is a formation of the unconscious. Although Lacan starts his conceptualisation of the symptom as a signifier (Lacan, 1953–4) and signification (Lacan, 1954–5), the clinic of neurotics challenged him to the extent that he was led to come up with another dimension to the concept of symptom formation, which offers a subject a mode of jouissance. The status of symptom changes from:

signifier → signification → metaphor (Lacan, 1966b) → enigmatic message (unrecognisable to the subject) (Lacan, 1960–1) → mode of jouissance/ mode of being → sinthome (beyond any meaning) (Lacan, 1975–6)

Over the years spanning 1953 to 1975, the concept of symptom formation traverses the dialectic of signifiers. As Lacan moves away from structuralism and linguistics, topological representation shows how symptom formation was calling out for a further interpretation in his later teaching. A subject's mode of being – or lack of being – finds resolution through her or his symptom, offering the subject a particular mode of enjoyment.

Such a view considers the question of the direction of treatment, as well as theorising the end of treatment. In psychoanalysis, we do not aim to decipher or decode a symptom as our ultimate goal but try to pinpoint the mode of jouissance a subject gets from it. The symptom – as a unique style of living for each subject – is, with the support of fantasy, gradually circumscribed through the work of analysis. The position of the analyst, therefore, elevates and maintains the status of the symptom in the Real. By handling an analysand's demands and pushing them to a desire to not understand, it is hoped that s/he will read the transcript of the symptom beyond significations and phallic metaphors. Early in the work, an analysand might be keen to ask the analyst: "So, in your opinion, why do I leave men as soon as they want to settle down or want a baby with me?" One possible way to approach such a demand for knowledge would be to acknowledge or reject it – regardless of how much truth is in it for the subject. Or, instead, to make the function of the analytical work about the mode of jouissance gained through such a pattern, by simply underlining "leaving" and "settling down" through "wanting a baby". The position of the analyst would not be reduced to a provider of solid knowledge and meaning, mortifying the analysand's burgeoning desire. The analyst facilitates a further elaboration of a symptomatic pattern instead of orienting the work solely around compensating for a Symbolic lack in a subject (castration). Hence, the analysand is pushed towards the Real of sexual non-rapport (Lacan, 1969–70).

The hysteric subject is attentive to the Other's desire and her strategy is to keep the Other's desire alive (Fink, 1997). So then, it would not be surprising if a hysteric subject sought some sort of challenge in her relationship with a partner who is "too predictable". It certainly requires special attention for an analyst to work through, for example, the symptomatic affairs or choices of hobbies of a hysteric in a committed relationship. In one case, a hysteric woman had a long-term relationship with a man who was uninterested in any personal hobbies other than being fully dedicated to his work and his wife. The hysteric subject did not seem to be bothered in her relationship, which sounded "boring" from the outside. The husband was a master of setting up surprises for his wife – the hysteric subject – as dedicated to his wife as much as he was to his work. They had a relationship that – although on a level of sexual non-rapport – revolved around an activity (to surprise and to be surprised) with two different functions that served two different, separate modes of jouissance. The hysteric wife was relating to the surprises as a medium to measure up her husband's desire for her (as being an object of her husband's desire) while her husband's symptom was his wife. She was, in fact, translating a mode of jouissance for him in the Real by being engaged in his games of surprises. We could also wonder about how his dedication to work had functioned for his wife's mode of jouissance. His work involved doing very complicated tasks and decoding complexity. He was described as a "super genius" man in her words. We could associate her fascination with his mental power to the Other jouissance as a modality of jouissance in women. In fact, he was not solely a dedicated man to her but he was also a superman beyond her.

In another case, a female analysand had a long-term sexual fantasy (daydream) of seeing her husband in bed with another woman. In real life, however, she was tormented by crippling jealousy about "the other woman". After analysis interrupted her complaining mode, she eventually became able to recognise the connection between her jealousy of other women and getting sexual excitement from this sexual fantasy. This was realised at a moment in analysis when she was pushed beyond any interpretation – as producing a meaning – of her symptom. The object of the drive was identified, linking the symptom to the Real of the body. A gap in the harmony of the chain of significations was used in order to allow the subject to read an "unreadable", instead of filling the gap with another brick!

Many cases of obsessional neurosis whose arrangement of the symptom (which has served them in such a way that they remain self-sufficient in relation to the Other's desire) fails him, end up in analysis, hoping to return to the same pattern as soon as possible. Being puzzled by the analyst and the Other's desire is not their cup of tea; and usually getting back into their good old ways is the main demand they have of the work. Having suffered from a series of break-ups with women whom he believed he had treated with high regard, one subject had the question of "why"; however, he started the work by pointing the finger of blame at the Other – as being unfaithful or ungrateful. Through different modes of intervention, the aim of analysis was to overcome the subject's reluctance around giving up his rigid relation towards knowledge, which was loved and valued for producing a meaning. Interpreting the Other's – his women's – desires as demands based on his assumptions about them was in fact his structural strategy. Eventually, what he desired from his relationships with women got a chance to be expressed. Apparently, he wanted to create a family but could not bear any potential partner's terms and conditions. He wanted a family that did not include him as a decision-maker. His usual choice of women who occupied a managerial position at work was a way to have someone who could rule his household as well as him. This was his symptomatic solution; but the work continued to elaborate on why such a position was taken by the subject in the first place. What mode of jouissance was offered to the subject in such an arrangement?

For an analysand whose response to a cut in sessions was to take out her e-cigarette almost immediately (in her words: "to carry on the mode of oral drive"), a constant change in manifestations of the symptom, with almost no interruption from one to the next was, in fact, her symptom. She had moved uninterruptedly in her symptoms; from eating problems to obsessive cleaning to sexual difficulties, following a loss. She benefited from a cut in sessions in order to question her inability to be interrupted, more precisely, to be interrupted from what was being aimed at.

So, the ways in which we make a clinical diagnosis in analysis, as well as in the treatment of a symptom, radically differ from medical approaches. In fact, elaborating on the subject's relation to her/his symptom not only gives clues about the underlying structure, it helps the subject to choose a different mode of being or symptom which proves less troubling. The manifestation of the symptom can be similar in hysteria and obsessional neurosis. Therefore, it can sometimes be a challenge for a clinician to make a differential diagnosis. It is only by going beyond what lies on the surface that we can examine the ways in which the subject defines her/his "non-being"; a strategy to approach a Symbolic lack, a desire for an object – object a – and a coming-to-terms with a "manque-à-être" – as Lacan defined it – (Lacan, 1958a) that one can eventually come to a diagnosis, so that we can move forward with the work, from lack to jouissance.

A scientific breakthrough for a scientist, jokes for a stand-up comedian, a novel for a writer or a story for a journalist: these all offer a subject a mode of living with a symptom as long as they can enjoy it. Otherwise, a subject is compelled to search for compensation. To be more precise, one cannot live without a symptom: having or not having routines and chores, being or not being part of different groups, belonging to or opting out of a trend, wanting or not wanting a relationship with the Other, learning a certain expertise or knowledge in a hobby or craft, responding to or ignoring an interruption in the continuity of everyday life, losing in order to find or remain lost in a specific mode of being, the position from which one chooses to speak, patience and impatience towards the Other; these are clearly not conscious formations produced by the Ego & Co.!

Symptom/synth-homme

So, what is a sinthome, as the fourth ring that knots together RSI (Real, Symbolic, Imaginary), in psychosis? In Seminar 23, Lacan, a fan of James Joyce's writing from his youth, refers to Joyce's self-recreation through a refashioning of language (Lacan, 1975–6). His creative writing had created a synthetic man (synth-homme). It had enabled him to punctuate, somehow, the intrusion of jouissance. Therefore, he had a new way to use imposed language. Regardless of how rightly or wrongly Lacan's diagnosis of Joyce's psychical structure was, the idea would still be valid if we think of a psychotic's constantly striving to create themselves or build new systems by which to live.

Working with their psychosis, many patients are able to trade in the Symbolic order by means of self-made constructions. A manic-depressive subject served in the role of consultant for governments in developing countries. The type of activities involved in his professional role were to nurture and sustain a mode of "constant" creativity and "rapid" change: the two main signifiers that functioned at the level of organising his volatile mode of jouissance. What had led him to see an analyst was an interruption in these work routines. He had returned to the UK and was asked to work in an office. He certainly did not want to be pinned down to a chair – as became evident during sessions, too. An inability to maintain even a short conversation with others, hypersexuality and non-stop binge eating was the picture of his symptomology at the time. To this subject, keeping at a distance from the Other meant to go as far away as possible, in a geographical sense. Being in proximity to his family and friends in the UK meant ending in big fights. He was highly functional and less troubled in his manic phase as opposed to his depressive mood, which was an extremely low one. During the work, it became clearer that nothing more than a professional position and achievement as a creative consultant could punctuate and deflate an excessive jouissance in him. In other words, we could say that his career was his sinthome as the fourth ring in a Lacanian Borromean knot which made his being more coherent. He had an identity as a consultant and has a purpose in life in helping others to reach their goals.

Conclusion

The mode of jouissance is free for a subject to explore only after she goes beyond the interpretation of identification with the Other's desire. This is when she formulates an answer – somehow – to the deal made between the subject and her Other. Once the subject is more able to confront the enigma of her being beyond the fantasy's conventional construction, then, through the elaboration of the symptomatic pattern, all the meaning (as knowledge) and the Symbolic dimension of language dissipate, and the subject eventually admits the mode of enjoyment she gets from the symptom. The subject is then free to be, or to have a choice.

Besides being a desiring subject, or perhaps being protected against the drive through the differing faces of desire, a parlêtre is a parlêtre when she has a body to objectify it: to make it an essential medium for enjoyment: to enjoy her being through or by it. We make our body fat, thin; we paint it, tan it, sell it, and reproduce ourselves by it. Although in cases of psychosis, "body" can be rather an abstract concept: "it is a bag of bones and blood"; "it is a sex machine"; "it is a drug store"; "it is a mannequin" or "it is a hanger" etc., the jouissance at the level of the body is there – though of course unorganised and in excess – for the subject, and s/he has to master it.

Lacanian "savoir-y-faire", which means knowing what to do with one's symptom (Lacan, 1975–6), happens after de-phallicising the object. The brilliance of the object is gone and the subject has come to terms with a limitation or a lack as castration. This is when the effect of "Lalangue" is a bit more readable and the subject knows what to do with it. The sinthome is constructed and is not reducible any more to a meaning. The change is there, but no more changing! A particular mode of jouissance would not be eliminable any more. This savoir-y-faire is not a "master" knowledge but yet, in the Real of the body, you are the captain of your soul and the master of your fate (*Invictus*).

It is a kind of still life. The stillness, the silence of the narrative, which was once, at the beginning, so full-on. At the end, after reading the invisible scripts of jouissance on the body, after there is not any further reading or writing, the symptom as a cause of malaise will be replaced by the sinthome about which the subject does not complain.

Bibliography

Fink, B. (1997). *A Clinical Introduction to Lacanian Psychoanalysis*. Cambridge, MA & London: Harvard.

Freud, S. (1886–1899). Letter 105 to Fliess, Dated 19 Feb 1899. In: J. Strachey, ed., *The Standard Edition of the Complete Psychological Works of Sigmund Freud, Vol 1*, p. 278. London: Vintage, 2001.

Freud, S. (1893–1899). The neuro-psychosis of defence, 1894. In: J. Strachey, ed., *The Standard Edition of the Complete Psychological Works of Sigmund Freud, Vol 3*, pp. 43–68. London: Vintage, 2001.

Freud, S. (1909). Two case histories: "Little Hans and The Rat Man". In: J. Strachey, ed., *The Standard Edition of the Complete Psychological Works of Sigmund Freud, Vol X*, pp. 3–149. London: Vintage, 2001.

Freud, S. (1911–1913). Case history of Schreber. In: J. Strachey, ed., *The Standard Edition of the Complete Psychological Works of Sigmund Freud, Vol XII*, pp. 3–82. London: Vintage, 2001.

Freud, S. (1916–1917). The sense of symptom. In: J. Strachey, ed., *The Standard Edition of the Complete Psychological Works of Sigmund Freud, Vol XVI*, pp. 257–272. London: Vintage, 2001.

Freud, S. (1917–1919). From the history of an infantile neurosis. In: J. Strachey, ed., *The Standard Edition of the Complete Psychological Works of Sigmund Freud, Vol XVII*, pp. 3–123. London: Vintage, 2001.

Freud, S. (1924). The ego and the id. In: J. Strachey, ed., *The Standard Edition of the Complete Psychological Works of Sigmund Freud, Vol XIX*, pp. 3–66. London: Vintage, 2001.

Freud, S. (1925–6). Inhibition, symptom and anxiety. In: J. Strachey, ed., *The Standard Edition of the Complete Psychological Works of Sigmund Freud, Vol XX*, pp. 77–174. London: Vintage, 2001.

Lacan, J. (1953–4). *The Seminar of Jacque Lacan: Book1: Freud's Paper on Technique*. John Forrester (Trans). New York & London: Norton.

Lacan, J. (1954–5). *The Seminar of Jacque Lacan: Book 2: The Ego in Freud's Theory and in the Technique of Psychoanalysis*. Sylvana Tomaselli (Trans). New York & London: Norton.

Lacan, J. (1960–1). *Le Séminaire Livre VIII: Le Transfert*. Paris: Seuil.

Lacan, J. (1966a). *Écrits:The Function and Field of Speech and Language (1953)*, pp. 237–268. Bruce Fink (Trans). New York & London: Norton.

Lacan, J. (1966b). *Écrits:The Instance of the Letter in the Unconscious, or Reason Since Freud (1957)*, pp. 412–455. Bruce Fink (Trans). New York & London: Norton.

Lacan, J. (1966c). *Écrits:The Direction of Treatment and the Principles of Its Power (1958a)*, pp. 489–542. Bruce Fink (Trans). New York & London: Norton.

Lacan, J. (1966d). *Écrits:The Signification of the Phallus (1958b)*, pp. 575–584. Bruce Fink (Trans). New York & London: Norton.

Lacan, J. (1969–70). *Le séminaire XVII: L'envers de la psychanalyse.* J.-A. Miller (Ed). Paris: Seuil, 1991: 134.

Lacan, J. (1975–6). *Le Séminaire Livre XXIII: Le Sinthome.* Paris: Seuil.

Chapter 5

Founder and inventor

Hysteria and obsessional neurosis

Introduction

All three of the terms of *hysteria*, *obsessional* and *neurosis* are generally considered to be politically loaded. While a trainee in psychoanalysis would be familiar with the concept of *neurosis*, and might even get anxious with not being diagnosed with either *hysteria* or *obsessional neurosis* in her personal analysis, the same is certainly not the case for a member of the public who would not infer the same connotations from the aforementioned terms. If, at a dinner party you forget that the rest of the guests are not familiar with psychoanalytical jargon, and use – accidentally – any of those words to describe a "normal" person, you might get yourself into trouble. When, while having a conversion with a passionate feminist, you decide to impress her with your smart talk and suddenly the term *hysteria* coughs up, rest assured that you will receive a raised eyebrow: "So, you think women are all hysterics?" Before you make a move to try to clarify the matter a bit by explaining that there are in fact both female and male versions of *hysteria*, not only have you made the subject more complicated, her defensiveness against what you had wished to say may then be too weighted against you to be overcome. Perhaps the smartest response would be what an obsessional neurotic might do: stopping right there and playing dead!

In our dinner party vignette, it would be just our analyst's luck to intrigue a nearby male guest, overhearing the exchange, and then entering the conversation to say: "So, eventually you invented a male version to keep things balanced."

Psychoanalysts are as aware of changes in current social discourse as others in the field. There is a change of attitude towards what makes a woman or a man – both individually and in relation to each other. Today, psychoanalysts are faced with more and more obsessional neurotic women in their clinic, just as they have been receiving an increasing number of male hysterics in the last decade or so, compared with numbers in the late twentieth century.

In psychoanalysis, the psychical structures are quite different from concepts such as gender identity. House-husbands, women running political office or functioning as ruling strategists in big corporations and the banking system: all now raise far fewer eyebrows than in the past. The question of gender equality in all social rights – beyond appearances or stereotypes – is now a matter that is becoming focused on and discussed much more widely than before. It is often approached as personal preference rather than purely socio-political question: more precisely, a subject's own choice. Hence, it causes far less surprise for the general public, which seems to have accepted subsequent change to a greater extent than ever before. For example, the fact that a father can look after his baby and enjoy spending his time with her more than his office work may contradict the stereotype of fatherhood, yet is widely accepted. Indeed, in many places around the world, we find "baby changing" rooms located outside the Ladies.

In psychoanalysis, the question of gender is approached in terms that go beyond the concept of identity. It is linked to a subject's separation and alienation from the Other (Lacan, 1963–4) and it is discussed in the context of "sexual non-rapport" (Lacan, 1969–70). The sub-categories of neurosis are perceived as concepts different from male or female sexualities, which are elaborated upon as either male virility or the "non-existing position" for *The woman*. Therefore, there are both male and female versions of the two psychical structures.

But why is there so much sensitivity around the concept of *hysteria, obsession* and *neurosis*?

In the usual sense of the word – in pop culture – *hysteria* means to be unruly, unpredictably excited and, more precisely, to be far away from being and acting "reasonably". It means being out of control. It is as if *hysteria* is a contagious condition – such as the "mass hysteria" discussed in sociology – or a sort of bad behaviour, which nobody likes to be described as having.

Neurosis also has a different meaning in everyday usage from what we find in the theory and clinic of psychoanalysis. In conversation with a friend, a psychoanalyst might find herself saying: "Oh! Totally neurotic", meaning that the person she is referring to is the most "normal" form of being that s/he could be; but it might be understood that she is referring to an anxious, maladjusted control freak. In fact, outside the realm of psychoanalysis, being neurotic means to possess certain traits, characteristics or behaviour which have more affinity with the obsessive pattern, which, of course, is not a compliment. A patient of mine used this term to describe her mother, who was actually paranoiac and stalked her (the patient's) father to his work almost every day. A so-called "neurotic" employer is one who does not trust his employee to carry out a task independently. He enjoys controlling their every move in order to adjust them to his own system – "my way or no way". This is interpreted as a neurotic form of management rather than being described more accurately as the perverse act that it is.

As for *obsessional neurosis*, this term could sometimes be seen as a positive trait. When, for example, someone is well-organised or has a passion in life: "I am obsessed with reading". Or, when someone says, "I am obsessed with you!" to mean "I love you passionately". Being an "obsessive" could sometimes imply perseverance, and a focus on achievement and success. I have had numerous analysands who wished to be diagnosed as an obsessional rather than being a hysteric. However, there is another side of the coin; if the obsession refers to certain symptoms such as obsessive cleaning or eating habits, then suddenly a doctor is needed. In particular, if the term is combined with other conditions such as compulsive behaviours or a depressive, anxious mood, it would then be considered as a clinical obsession needing treatment, from the point of view of some professionals in the field.

So, now you may help yourself to some of the unfriendly, uncanny jargon of psychoanalysis in the following pages but please be advised to refrain from using them at any dinner party you attend – unless you are ready to fight your way out at the cost of spoiling your evening.

Freud meets hysteria

When Freud started to formulate categories of diagnosis such as hysteria and obsessional neurosis, his clinical observations and research were the source for this conceptualisation. As early as 1888, in an article called "Hysteria", he challenged the idea, common from early civilization till his own time, of neurosis being linked with the female sexual apparatus (Freud, 1886–1889). Such an idea did not only concern the view of the general public, and professionals working on mental suffering were of the same opinion. In his earliest writing on hysteria, after he gave up the use of hypnosis, Freud considers *hysteria* as a physical illness – despite not having any supporting medical evidence on changes in the patient's nervous system. However, at this stage in his formation, according to James Strachey, Freud was still following Charcot's doctrine in his approach to *hysteria*. He gradually developed his own independent ideas about *hysteria*. It would be worth working further on this very early text of Freud's in order to get a sense of how *hysteria* as a separate diagnosis sprang from psychiatric texts, to land up in the world of psychoanalysis, where it has since been worked through, over and over again.

Here, in this text, Freud describes *hysteria* as a "physio-pathological" illness, not a "neurological" disease. Unlike some of his neurologist peers, who still to this day consider the aetiology of seizure and convulsion in patients to be a neurological defect, he noticed a group of patients had convulsive attacks, which were precipitated alongside peculiar auras which showed no evidence of brain-related damage or defects. He concluded with a diagnosis: *hysteria*. To this day, in hospital triage, convulsion is a matter of discussion in terms of whether to refer it to the neurological or psychiatric wards. At first, Freud went into great scrutiny of the peculiar condition known as *hysteria*, trying to evaluate it. As you can read in his early writings on the subject, he describes the three phases of a hysterical attack as being very similar to an epileptic attack. He also described the hallucinations and coma that in some severe cases followed the attack:

- Aura was mainly around the throat, temples, ears and could be accompanied by a sense of having a lump in the pharynx.
- The attack may have a "grand arching movement" similar to an epileptic attack.

Regarding the localisation of the hysterical attack in the body – hysterogenic zones – Freud distinguishes female *hysteria* from the male version: the female patient suffers from the condition mainly around the trunk and upper and lower extremities, while the male patient's symptoms are focused around his testes and spermatic cord. It is thought-provoking to learn about how Freud distinguished his female and male patients' symptomology based on clinical observation of bodily expression. Such an observation is still valid in the modern clinic for male and female patients complaining of psychosomatic symptoms in their bodies. In the same text, Freud differentiates between seizures caused by actual neurological defects and the physio-pathology of *hysteria* by referring to the existence of hyper- or hypo-sensitivity toward temperature or air pressure on certain sense organs (the skin, eyes, ears and nose) in hysteric patients. One could also wonder about the concept of the drive in relation to different manifestations of *hysteria*. After all, the way in which each subject enjoys her/his mode of being does not exclude the existence of the body.

When you receive a patient complaining of, for example, a bizarre sensation somewhere in the body, the partial paralysis of a limb, a complaint of bowel or bladder functions, such as cystitis or irritable bowel syndrome, or perhaps a constantly changing food allergy or intolerance with no organic causes found, would you think of *hysteria* straightaway? I would not. Instead, one might want to learn more about the underlying question for the subject who suffers from a certain symptom in her/his body.

In a case I received a while ago, one of the patient's finger joints was deformed with an outward inclination, with similar signs to those of rheumatoid arthritis (RA) – an auto-immune disorder. Not a single medical test or examination indicated such a disorder but the patient was sure of her illness. She initially came to seek help for her panic attacks and insomnia, but in the first consultation I was struck by her hand deformity. With my medical mind, I had the same first impression of RA; but she told me that her test results did not indicate that diagnosis. She spoke of pains in her body in the context of complaining about her anxious mood. The flow of that first consultation took another turn after my question – out of pure curiosity – regarding her hand. Now, she spoke of her anxiety, pain and deformed hands. She continued with her idea of the possibility of having inherited a congenital condition in her hands. Her father, who had suffered from multiple sclerosis, had died in a car accident at almost the same age as she was now. Around the same time, she was tormented by unexplained anxiety attacks.

Well, without rushing into making an interpretation regarding an identification with her father, as Freud's early work would suggest, or concluding it is a hysterical attack, as the medical interpretation might dictate, much more scrutiny was needed in this case. Why the identification with her father's potentially life-threatening condition? Why the localisation of pain and deformity in her hand? These were fundamental questions to be explored. Since when, and in which context had she become ill? Next, her relationship with men became the main focus of the work: searching for love and not being chosen as the love of someone's life. And now the traces of hand deformity were found in an expression in her mother tongue: "not being taken seriously" or "not being trusted" due to having deformed hands and feet. This is a literal translation of the expression in English, which she had heard throughout her childhood. This process took almost four years while, over those years, she complained about her hand deformity preventing her from doing things that she enjoyed. After that moment in the work, she noticed she could make use of her hands again. Her unconscious had interpreted her mother's equivocal expression literally in the Real body as having deformed hands.

In this case of *hysteria*, the question of interpretation contradicted the early psychoanalytical interpretation of symptom formation and the identification with the father. Beyond the theme of identification with the Other, a subject's agency in choosing a position was what was targeted. The work certainly did not focus only on manifestations of the symptom, or revolve around un-repressing a repressed wish. It was oriented more towards the subject's positioning in relation to the Other's desire: why she identified with what her mother had described her as. At the early stages of psychoanalysis, however, the aim of clinical investigation was mainly concerned with the manifestations of the symptom as a way to make a differential diagnosis. Such manifestations can also be found in psychosis.

In another case, a young woman and mother-of-two was complaining of facial hemi-paraesthesia, a pins-and-needles sensation on one side of her face, with a bit of oedema. On further investigation of her symptomology, it appeared that her so-called hysterical, psychosomatic symptoms were associated with pregnancy; to be more precise, with her desire to have a child and not only one, but two. In Freud's early texts, this patient's symptom was referred to as paralysis and paraesthesia of a hysterical body, involving the complaint of "hemiplegia" or "paraplegia". Without any assumed knowledge, I tried to explore beyond a descriptive picture of her condition. I never got a chance to understand exactly why pregnancy, why her feminine position and why the number two, which all seemed particular to her case. She never came back but emailed me a short time later and thanked me for making the nuisance disappear. The miracle of psychoanalysis! Her unconscious seemed to have interpreted my intervention. I had only gently pinpointed the above elements in her narrative.

Freud described in detail the nature of hysterical muscular contracture in his own time. The dramatic, arching movements of a hysterical attack back then remind us of images of convulsive attacks. Fainting was also another common manifestation of *hysteria*. The question here, then, would be why we do not see such dramatic scenes in the clinic of *hysteria* today. The famous scene in the movie *The Exorcist* is a close enough example of a depiction of a hysterical attack from those theatrical days even if, a 360-degree head rotation might seem an exaggeration.

If we agree on a couple of points here regarding *hysteria*, we might have an explanation for the prevalence of such descriptions of the illness back then. Firstly, many historical cases of *hysteria* are now considered to be cases of psychosis. Many manifestations of *hysteria* are only an envelope for a hidden psychotic structure, and vice versa. If a clinician digs into the details of the case, the question of the Other's desire, the division of the subject and the manifestation of jouissance can help in making a diagnosis. Copying the other in psychosis, in a rather abstract, simple way, contradicts the more complicated identification with the Other's desire supported by fantasy in neurosis. The imitation and copying of the idea of the other's illness is particularly evident in schizophrenia. In hysteria, we have the identification with the Other's desire after recognising a symbolic lack as castration in the Other. Many analysts describe this as a "chameleon" strategy (Verhaeghe, 2004). As such, we might have an answer to our riddle: the prevalence of convulsive attacks was quite high due to the lack of treatment in the late nineteenth century.

A hysterical subject can orchestrate his or her clinical picture towards what is trending in the society in which s/he lives. For example, in the early years of the 2000s, there was a surge of so-called bipolar disorders everywhere in the media and talk shows with celebrities boosting their fame upon diagnosis, and loads of research projects on the subject funded by drug manufacturers in order to promote their products. Psychiatrists were compulsively diagnosing many patients with different variations of names for this classification – from hypo-mania and bipolar type II to full-blown bipolarity – in their clinics. Many cases that were diagnosed as bipolar were, in fact, simply hysteric or schizophrenic subjects with non-pathological elevated mood.

In *Dangerous Method*, a movie exploring the relationship between Jung, Freud and Sabina Spielrein in the early years of psychoanalysis, the portrayal of Spielrein is considered as a case of *hysteria* whose transference to Jung made her go on to study medicine and psychoanalysis. Almost 20 years after Freud wrote his paper on *hysteria*, she becomes unwell following her sister's death. Jung, Bleuler's assistant at the time, brings her back on track, to such an extent that she acts as his assistant in a research study. The miracle of such an intense transference – referred to as a poetic relationship in a letter to her mother, then a physical passion, as confessed to Freud (Lothane, 1999) – enabled her to function from a position of a "helper" rather than only being seen as a patient. Her intelligence and effort helped her to become one of the first female psychoanalysts in the history of psychoanalysis. After a short time, she recovers from her so-called hysterical attacks. A new ideal image acting as her compass in life motivates her to study medicine, the year following her admission to the psychiatric ward in Zurich. In this case history, her masochistic fantasy – being beaten and getting sexual pleasure from it – seems to be related to the subject's sexuality rather than a structural position towards the Other's lack. In those early years of psychoanalysis, the two concepts seemed not to be distinguished. In the same way, many early clinical case histories of hysteria are in fact those of psychotic subjects. Emma Eckstein is another so-called hysteric in a case which, based on today's analysis of the concept, is now considered as psychosis.

Was there any question regarding the Other's desire in the clinic of those so-called hysterical patients? In fact, the focus of the work was only concerned with a dyadic relationship between trauma and effect. So, it is not surprising why some feminists of the time – and still to this day – without fully grasping the concept of *hysteria*, criticise it for being a discriminating concept against women. Even the choice of the term is unwelcome, as if "hysteria" meant "madness". Cross my heart, they are not the same in psychoanalysis! The questioning of sexuality is a common feature of the clinic of *hysteria*, but the psychical structure is not the same as the sexual position of *The woman*, which Lacan elaborated on to a greater extent. However, he was misunderstood and misinterpreted in his controversial comment: "*The woman* does not exist!" (Lacan, 1969–70).

Towards the end of the early article on *hysteria*, Freud finds – somehow – his own feet as "Dr Freud", not a Charcotian disciple. He identifies the hysterical complaint with two further characteristics: excessiveness and ignoring the laws of science, the nervous and psychical systems. In his own words: "changing ideas, inhibition of the activity of will, magnification and suppression of feelings" (Freud, 1886–1889, p. 49). Such characteristics can also be found in other psychical structures. However, if it concerns a hysterical subject, such manifestations can be understood as a structural positioning towards the object causing desire: *objet a*, in relation to the Other (Fink, 1997). A change in ideas and a newfound motivation to do certain types of activities may involve the hysteric tendency towards attentiveness to the desire of the Other. An enigma, which should be figured out.

In today's practice of psychoanalysis, in the epoch of speed and speedy satisfaction, "changeable" does not convey the same meaning as in the late nineteenth century. Possessing such a tendency can even be interpreted as a sign of intelligence, success, or extraordinary capacity in life. One businessman had a new idea for his business almost every day, after a revelation each morning. By the end of the day, that morning's idea had already expired. Continuity and repetition were not his cup of tea, and being in a steady job meant the end of the world. However, this subject's structural position did not imply a male *hysteria*. When anything can be just one click away in terms of availability of options – to promptly be or have such-and-such – we have come to know that *hysteria* has a high risk of becoming contaminated by trends: the poor hysterical subjects of today!

Besides the question of desire, sexuality in *hysteria* is not the same as in Freud's time. We are not in the 1960s' version of sexuality either: it is not merely a reactionary response to repressed or suppressed sex. Such a question should not be approached only from the perspective of sexism and gender equality. At least, this is not the type of approach we choose to take in psychoanalysis.

Freud, in this paper, continues with his clinical observation of *hysteria*: hysterics, he says, are prone to certain hereditary illnesses (Freud, 1886–1889). How could such an idea be considered with regards to *hysteria* as a structure in our own, contemporary time? Let us take the example of the localisation of the symptomology of *hysteria* in the body, the existence of some non-organic illnesses running in the family from previous generations. There will always be the echo of a hysteric desire originating in the field of the Other in such clinical speculation. Hysterics are attentive to the Other's desire. They identify with such a desire through a dialectical relation with the Other. Not all hysterics in a certain clan share the same master signifier to represent them to the Other (Lacan, 1963–4). The fantasy scenario that supports desire takes the form of different missions in life for each hysteric subject.

In *hysteria* with physical complaints, this is an essential point to be elaborated on in the clinic of psychoanalysis. Not only can such complaints say something about a hysteric's desire, but other elements such as the subject's drive, and the mode of jouissance associated with it, can also be delineated through such an investigation. There will not be a direct relation between the physical symptomology and the so-called family drama. Nor will they all suffer in the same pattern, in the body, the Real of the body which has escaped signification and any symbolisation. The body bears testimony to the effect of the Other's discourse after a subjective twist. The pattern of an illness, finding an expression in the body, can be a helpful lead towards the subject's choice of position.

In one case, a young female subject was complaining about her diagnosed ME, myalgic encephalomyelitis, which she had had since turning 18. Her main complaint was being almost always tired and insomniac. She could not cope with her sore throat and an intermittent electrical sensation in her spine any more. Her grandfather had been executed during a revolution. He was hanged. This grandfather was an army officer who had rescued many soldiers by carrying them on his back over a battlefield. Furthermore, he was the eldest of five children to whom he had served as a father figure and breadwinner. From the burden of his family to the weight of others soldiers' bodies, his life had been brutally ended by a rope around his neck. Why on earth had this life story found a means of expression in the body of a girl two generations later, once she turned 18? The thread of trauma from the past was destined to lead to the future, and the start of the unpleasant manifestations at the age 18 resembles somehow the Sleeping Beauty fairy tale. However, unlike the princess, this girl was unable to sleep well and her rescue did not lie in the kiss of a Prince Charming. Rather, it was in her own possession and she fought her mode of suffering during an unsettling journey through analysis. In this work, the interpretation was certainly not confined to the theme of identification with a father figure or the return of the repressed or trans-generational guilt. Rather, the subject was pushed towards a highly detailed consideration of the localisation and inscription of jouissance in her body. This enabled the subject to read the effect of the trauma and eventually liberated her from the Other. The work was conducted between the Symbolic and the Real, to extract the Real of the trauma as much as language allowed the subject to do this. The marks of analytic discourse made it possible for this subject to work through the nonsensical sensations in her body.

Obsessional neurosis

Freud arrives at the concept of "trauma" in this very early paper on hysteria. Although he does not elaborate the question of trauma and the inception of neurosis here in depth, he refers to the outbreak of neurosis – in both men and women – at a certain age. For Freud, the earliest manifestation of neurosis would be between the age of 6 and 10 in both sexes, but with more prevalence in girls, and again, during adolescence, which used to be a common age for marriage, back in those days. He links this observation to the subject's sexual life. Later, he distinguishes the two types of neurosis, *hysteria* and *obsessional neurosis*, as based on early trauma and repression, respectively; the former having had too little pleasure, while the latter having had too much of a certain pleasure (Freud, 1893–1899). This results in disgust in *hysteria* and guilt in *obsessional neurosis*, coinciding with the initial positioning of the subject towards the first significant Other, based on their interpretation of jouissance and excitement. In the second positioning, the *hysteric* reproaches the other, while the *obsessional neurotic* diverts the reproach towards himself. However, in Freud's works it is the symptomology of the neurosis that differentiates the two, rather than the positioning of the subject and the Other.

In *obsessional neurosis*, there is an urgency to repeat certain rituals. The person might complain for years about coming to analysis, yet keep coming back every week. The motif of such complaints is different from enjoying the act of nagging. As early as his third seminar, Lacan considers an obsessional neurotic as a subject with an existential question: am I dead or alive (Lacan, 1955–6)? Such a question is formulated in relation to the Other's lack. The question at stake is the obsessional's strategy to ward off his lack and to justify his existence in relation to the Other. This is one possible way to choose, in order to escape, the liveliness of the Other's desire (Fink, 1997). It might take him a good few years to eventually come face-to-face with his desiring Other without being unsettled by such a confrontation, and trying either to play dead or to mortify any trace of live desire coming from the field of the Other.

The motif of being in debt in relation to the Other described in the Ratman case (Freud, 1909) comes from a feeling of guilt associated with a wish for the Other's death. He had irrational anxiety in relation to his girlfriend and his father, linked with a possible threat to their wellbeing. Therefore, the Ratman was entangled in a torturous, compulsive repetition in his symptomology. It is rather a common complaint in the clinic of obsessional neurosis to hear about their helplessness in avoiding certain sets of rituals preventing them from moving on. If they ever decide to move on from the symptom that they have formed, then we could wonder what was at stake for the subject's jouissance in such rigidity. According to Lacan in his eighth seminar, the obsessional neurotic tends to turn the gift to faeces and then himself into faeces (Lacan, 1960–1). What did he mean by this conclusion?

The guiding motto behind an obsessional's rituals is a rigid logic, as rigid as the question of life and death. To change their approach to everyday life is almost impossible in some cases, no matter how much they might lose or pay a price for taking such a position. For an obsessional subject, having a radical belief in logical thinking and reasoning, and being obsessed with the structure of scientific discourse and the law, can act as a temporary anxiety-reducer. Until, that is, all his strategies, which were in fact set up so as to avoid loss, end in a big loss. A loss that can no longer be compensated for by his symptom. The pitfall in this structure is that, even through the treatment, the rigidity regarding not letting go of the symptom prevents the subject from being able to listen to what is said, even in his own narratives in analysis which aim to reduce the Other's desire to a demand.

An obsessional neurotic started psychoanalysis in order to treat his overwhelming anxiety, caused by not meeting the Other's deadlines at work. He was always late in delivering the tasks he was assigned, to the extent that he was on the verge of being fired. He had already received a few clinical diagnoses from outside psychoanalysis, ranging from Anxiety Disorder to Chronic Fatigue Syndrome. Lack of energy and motivation had even made him consider suicide. Making the journey to my consulting room, which only involved a 30-minute commute, seemed to be so much work that he was demanding phone sessions: "I'm afraid not!" I replied "The journey is essential." The differential diagnoses regarding this particular case initially seemed to be between melancholia and obsessional neurosis. However, it did not take a long time till the question of structure became clear. The subject said that he would have an easier life if he was not ordered to submit his assigned projects to a certain deadline. He was certainly concerned with his health, as well as his social relationships. Who he was for the Other, and, more precisely, his value for others around him had a strong and confusing significance for this subject, unlike what we find in melancholia. However, the way in which he had formulated the Other's desire was different from a hysteric's question. Not meeting a deadline could be due to the fact that a subject wants to set his own deadline, outside the law of the Other, as a way to mortify or neutralise it. Hysterics do not risk the impossible exchange of the Other's desire for liveliness by deadening it. In *hysteria*, the Other's desire is wanted alive and kicking!

In the above case, material related to his childhood revealed that he was apparently gifted in drawing landscapes. His parents had decided to give him a small amount of money for each drawing as an encouraging gesture. In an early vignette, he remembered having episodes of constipation and spending over an hour on the toilet. His mother's solution was to give him a piece of paper and a pencil to carry on drawing there, in order not to get bored. He had then discovered an enjoyment in defecating and drawing simultaneously. He was producing two shits but being paid for which one? What was his interpretation of this suggestion coming from the Other? Why did he have a dilemma in delivering tasks on time at work? He seemed to have succeeded in turning himself into faeces, while getting attention as someone who would delay finishing his work. But why did he not pursue the drawing? The above questions were to be explored beyond a classical interpretation of the equivalences of his wage, gift and shit! In his personal life with women, he had a position almost like a prostitute. The women he dated were all wealthy and payed for his expenses. The status of the knowledge produced in analysis did not seem to be his favourite thing, as this was not given to him. He was, however, pushed further in his understanding of the actual cause of his problem within the Symbolic order, beyond a signifier.

The theme of procrastination in the clinic of an obsessional has a different meaning than in *hysteria*. Since a hysterical subject is cautious to formulate her/his desire, as s/he needs to evaluate and measure the Other's desire, it might take her/him a bit longer to accomplish her/his mission in doing so. The motif of procrastination in the obsessional patient is, on the contrary, due to a desire to silence the Other's desire. All his precautions are organised around this strategy, conducted in a measured way.

He is not so much in love with the game of passion in relation to the Other. He prefers to look just like everybody else around him, fading into the background. Or, perhaps, he simply does not care about being or looking different in a social context as much as a hysteric wants to. The amount of effort a hysteric might put into planning her self-presentation towards others is beyond comparison with an obsessional's level of concern here.

According to Lacan's Geneva conference on the symptom, the obsessional neurotic enjoys being, and even remaining, in his thoughts: the thoughts which carry on in a closed circuit (Lacan, 1975). His love of the Symbolic order keeps this closed-off register dear to him. Everything should be a signifier, end of conversation! Over and over again. This description of obsessional structure raises the question of differential diagnosis between obsessional neurosis and paranoia.

When we paint such a gloomy picture of the obsessional neurotic structure with its motifs of impossibility, mortification, lack of passion, death and faeces, we seem to have forgotten that being already dead is equated with being immortal, as Lacan said early in his work (Lacan, 1955–6). What else could he lose in this game with the Other? Moreover, he is balanced on both sides: doing nothing, as if he is waiting for a termination of the master sooner or later (Lacan, 1953).

Alternatively, he could never allow himself to stop repetition, as if he would die if he does not do so. In other words, he can be an over-doer in either direction. So, we would be wrong to think of a sloth when it comes to the structural position of an obsessional. He is, rather, a Mr Incredible; either he has the gifts of a superpower or he does not.

Bibliography

Fink, B. (1997). *A Clinical Introduction to Lacanian Psychoanalysis*. Cambridge, MA & London: Harvard.

Freud, S. (1886–1899). Pre-psychoanalytic publications. Hysteria. In: J. Strachey, ed., *The Standard Edition of the Complete Psychological Works of Sigmund Freud, Vol I*, pp. 39–59. London: Vintage, 2001.

Freud, S. (1893–1899). Early psychoanalytic publications. The neuro-psychoses of defence. In: J. Strachey, ed., *The Standard Edition of the Complete Psychological Works of Sigmund Freud, Vol III*, pp. 41–61. London: Vintage.

Freud, S. (1909). Two case histories: "Little Hans and The Rat Man." In: J. Strachey, ed., *The Standard Edition of the Complete Psychological Works of Sigmund Freud, Vol X*, pp. 153–249. London: Vintage, 2001.

Lacan, J. (1953). The Neurotic's Individual Myth. In: *Ornicar?*, 1979. J.A. Miller (Ed).

Lacan, J. (1955–6). *The Seminar of Jacques Lacan: Book III: The Psychoses*. J.-A. Miller (Ed), Russell Grigg (Trans). London: Routledge, 1993.

Lacan, J. (1960–1). *Le Séminaire Livre VIII: Le Transfert*. Paris: Seuil.

Lacan, J. (1963–4). *The Seminar of Jacque Lacan: Book XI: Four Fundamental Concepts of Psychoanalysis*. Alan Sheridan (Trans). New York & London: Norton.

Lacan, J. (1966). *Écrits: The Mirror stage as Formative of the I Function as Revealed in Psychoanalytic Experience (1953)*. Bruce Fink (Trans). New York & London: Norton, pp. 75–82.

Lacan, J. (1969–70). *Le séminaire XVII: L'envers de la psychanalyse*. J.-A. Miller (Ed). Paris: Seuil, 1991.

Lacan, J. (4th Oct 1975). *Geneva Lecture on the Symptom*. Russell Grigg (Trans). Published: Analysis no. I. Melbourne: Centre for Psychoanalytic Research, 1989. pp. 7–26.

Lothane, Z. (1999). Tender love and transference: Unpublished letters of CG Jung and Sabina Spielrein. *International Journal of Psychoanalysis*, 16: 12–27, 81–94.

Verhaeghe, P. (2004). *On Being Normal and Other Disorders: A Manual for Clinical Psychodiagnostics*. New York: Other Press.

Chapter 6

Is singularity near?

Reclaiming the subject of the drive in the era of singularity

Introduction

The alarm clock rings at 6.00 am. The smell of coffee welcomes an ordinary day. The best part of the morning is running through an almost empty park with some early-bird strangers passing by. The worst part of the morning however, is turning on my PC. A "bling!" and a flash of a flat screen, an email browser pops up. My virtual office, which has a blurred boundary now with my real office space, plans, instructs and marks my day. Now, even in my wildest dreams, I cannot avoid this "click", I cannot just keep running in nature. I cannot even pinpoint when it was that my morning's chores were hijacked by this. A binge reader of the previous night's book in the morning, I used to turn one page after another with one hand, a cup of coffee in the other and a radio programme playing in the background. I inherited such routines from my mother and she had taken it from her mother. Now, without being fully aware of such a change of routine, this new set has crept in to my much-loved mornings. I have replaced many tools with a screen. My body postures and movements have changed in order to be adjusted to them. If I want to push it a bit further, the boundary between my body and the technology is already undefinable.

Once, in a state of shock after realising how much I had become dependent upon my broadband connection and my new devices, I decided to cut them all out from my everyday life. Being so sure of my ability to return to the good old days, I went gadget-free, starting with my smart phone. In less than a few hours, I found myself lost, searching a street for a friend's home address – a friend whose telephone number was also wiped from my memory. Before boring you with all the hassles which I faced in the following few days of becoming a techno-luddite, a sort of techno-vegan, I was convinced that resisting this new era of technology is not only impossible but also rather stupid. We need these little bits and pieces of new technical tools in every aspect of our daily life – from the toilet seat to the bedside. I guess that we can agree that most of us are more dependent on our gadgets and the so-called virtual world than we have been on any other objects or spaces in the past. What is offered to the subject is a possibility, which is the constancy of an access. The subject is facing far fewer limitations that s/he had to before. We humans take pleasure in going beyond a limit. Paranoia and phobia of employing such technologies in our everyday life make us even more alienated from this new era and the fundamental changes that it has created at a super high speed.

Before making the direction of my argument in this chapter clear, I want to mention that the question of the subject's desire to create and employ new technologies, from information to robotics, can also be approached from the perspective of the question of power and phallic jouissance. In the domain of mega Information Technology (IT) corporations, such as Google, which obtain such an enormous power from the data gathered from users' behavioural patterns, the winner is the one who has greater and quicker access to this form of knowledge. We might wonder here about the concept of a subversive subject on the dark-web and the creation of bitcoin; Other jouissance and sexual non-rapport in the realm of online dating; the status of *objet a* and making choices in capitalistic online marketing; the question of the gaze and the "like"-mania around the image/profile, which reduces the Real of the Other's desire to a never-satisfied demand for real objects. They can all become a topic for discussion in the field of psychoanalysis. Social media, for example, has changed the nature of communication and gratification in a contemporary subject's social and personal life. Traversing certain limitations with which s/he was once faced in the past has, however, brought upon her/him a new form of limitation. The question of *how far* and *how much* privacy illustrates well one aspect of the contemporary subject's dilemma while surfing social media.

One could ask where is the limit between the virtual and real world when we reflect on the ideas of communication, friendship, relationship and sexual pleasure. The boundary is even more blurred once we reach this even newer epoch, beyond the world of smart phones and social media: the realm of AI – Artificial Intelligence. It has been a while since Siri was introduced into our iPhones. Now, you interact with your Alexa on a kitchen shelf: a newer and yet still primitive form of AI. You have been using AI without realising or acknowledging it long before Alexa played music for you on a rainy day. All digital recognition devices were employed using machine learning platforms. Self-driven cars, not yet legalised in the UK, are amazingly welcomed by daily commuters who have chosen driving as a mode of commuting. Someone might enjoy a weekend workshop – getting hands dirty – repairing and tuning up car engines (which I am personally a big fan of), or perhaps driving manual cars as a hobby but not really enjoying the everyday driving experience of queuing on a variable speed control motorway. Well, Tesla and BMW are now well advanced in this field.

My intention is neither to promote nor decry this new era. I am not warning readers of new changes, nor judging these changes as either constructive or destructive to a human subject's life. Rather, I want to pinpoint and explore the speed of such changes, resulting from advanced technologies, leaving us a limited space for further reflection and elaboration. After all, a compromise has already been made with this new lifestyle. Now, we are entering a newer version of virtual reality: AI, which is more Real than we have seen at any other time. Perhaps some of us would not take such a topic seriously when it is termed "cognitive intelligence" or a "computing" device. We might not wonder about such fields since, right from the beginning, they seem not to be relevant to the analytical discourse. Or perhaps it would be too simplistic to enter such a domain of the imaginary from a psychoanalytical perspective. I, personally, was not impressed by learning about IBM Watson, a supercomputer which knows about human knowledge so broadly and so swiftly that it gives an answer faster than any human would be capable of. A super intelligent master-mind version of any encyclopaedia! The reason that I became more and more interested in this field of expertise was precisely because of our – the psychoanalysts' – absence in contemporary debates around AI.

I started by questioning my own resistance towards the matter until eventually I was able to listen to this new discourse. The first thing that got my attention in such debates was the topic of logical thinking and decision making. An AI is believed to be able to process logical reasoning much quicker and more efficiently than a super intelligent human being. That was the moment which grabbed my attention, the moment at which I seized the issue. Decision making is a much more complicated task than pure logical calculation.

The AI is around the corner!

It is believed that a group of scientists from different fields, mainly from "Nanotechnologies", "Genetics" and "Robotics", have been busy creating a human robot, which is more efficient, has better health and more memory capacity in analysing available/given data than any human. These qualities would enable the robot to make predictions, thus becoming able to make better choices. A human robot, who should obtain civil rights. Let us temporarily put our fearful fantasies, immediate anger and rejection of the idea, aside. This is happening and will turn into an even more complicated matter if we miss the boat and do not start discussing the topic now.

Based on contemporary clinical practice, complaints concerning a subject's sex life, which in fact carries the question of sexuality, seem to be changing. The echo of the sexualised body has changed since the start of the third millennium both in the clinic of neurosis and psychosis. The dramatic pace of change, which is discussed in "The singularity is near" by well-known futurist Ray Kurzweil, might prevent a subject from feeling nostalgia for the distant past, and generate nostalgia for a time only 15 years ago, when the invention of Viagra revolutionised the quality of life for old men!

It was roughly 15 years ago when I received a middle-aged man in my medical practice requiring a prescription to help him regain his sex life. He described his condition by explaining that he used to have a high "libido" hungry for sex several times a night and now, not only had he lost his appetite for sexual intercourse, but satisfying his girlfriend seemed impossible to him. This had generated in him an enormous anxiety, which he could not cope with any longer. He wanted a prescription as a golden remedy to fix him. Although a bit of exploration nuanced his story of temporary impotence differently, he wanted it fixed as quickly as possible. He loved his girlfriend so much that he could not have sex with her. His obsessional strategy of keeping two objects as separated as possible, however, eventually found an opportunity for elaboration in an analytical rather than a medical framework.

Due to the changes in social discourses and cultural orientations around the question of sex, forms and the manifestations of complaints around sexual relations as well as sexual identity/ambiguity have traversed the problem of sexual intercourse in marital bedrooms, red-light districts or the porn industry, seen in campaigning about sexism, equal pay and the global "#MeToo" campaign.

What will happen to the Real of the body and sexuality a few decades from now? What awaits a human subject who has been transposed/uploaded to another flesh if this one day becomes possible (transcendence)? How would an AI differ from a repressed subject with a marked body? If an ill body of a subject can be replaced by machine parts with learned senses, what could we exchange for a human being today (a sentient robot in a post-biological era)?

In order to reach some possible answers to the above questions later in this chapter, I will give you an account of the drive from both Freud's and Lacan's understandings of the concept.

I have always been a fan of movies such as *The Matrix*, *Wall-E*, *Her*, *Transcendence* and *Ex Machina*. I have put the above movies' titles chronologically here, and for some who have watched them, the trend can be depicted as moving from internet creation to curiosity around AI. The film-makers' preoccupation with the field of IT is evolving from the communication and interaction with the Other of the machine, to becoming a machine, in other words, creating a super human. What is brought up in each of these movies in the field of information technology is widely discussed in different fields, from branches of philosophy and psychology to economics and politics. Psychoanalytically, however, we can approach the question from not only a broader angle but even from a different direction. What we will argue here will focus on the question of the body and the drive in contrast to machine learning and enhancing the quantity and quality of human intelligence. I am hoping to start a basic debate here on the subject for a much deeper and more detailed elaboration of the question in due course.

A while ago, at a dinner party, an AI specialist approached me knowing that I am a psychoanalyst. We had a good chat on the subject of singularity and IT. Ray Kurzweil's "The singularity is near" had recently been published. Although I did not agree with a single point he made during our chat, the discussion marked me, to the extent that I found myself reading and researching on robotics, mathematics and AI for hours and hours. I became fascinated with such topics, which seemed to be miles and miles away from my usual sources of interest. It was quite an experience. I could not stop thinking about it – even during my morning run which was a sacred time for me. In my fantasy, I started to become already nostalgic about what I was sensing from nature: the little ducklings, white swans and the green grass, would they remain real? As if I was identifying with Wall-E, an animated cartoon character, fascinated by folk dancers on a broken TV.

Well, I am pretty sure that I did not betray Freud's legacy nor disappoint Lacan's readers with their re-definition of psychoanalysis, the subject and her/his desire and drive, by believing something that we might be dismissive about in the world of psychoanalysis is happening and changing the world out there. I even became a bit concerned about the fate of psychoanalysis in the next few decades. According to Kurzweil, 2045 is the year when the singularity arrives. His argument is not that the human will become united with the machine of intelligence. Singularity is the point which cannot be defined by any mathematical calculation. The Real of this undefined point could be considered as a commercial debate which attracts attention or feeds many enjoyable fantasies. It causes a turmoil of excitement. However, what caught my attention was a discussion around an era which was referred to as "post-biological". This will not be an era of dependence upon our gadgets or connectivity of the internet, nor an age of confusion between reality and virtual realms. Rather this would be about a new form of human. I am not sure that using the term of machine-human or even artificially intelligent robots would describe the start of singularity. Scientists in the field believe that these human robots are healthier, with greater capacities for memory and imagination. The transcendence of human beings to a different body constitutes the post-biological era.

In my heated debate with the AI specialist, I was trying to make him question his understanding of human beings beyond the mind, as theorised in psychology, and the body, as theorised in medicine. I was trying to explain to him that Freud, more than a century ago, discovered the unconscious, and that many other great thinkers of the twentieth century elaborated upon his discoveries. Naively, I was trying to explain that the desire of a human subject, his complicated sexuality, regardless of his psychical structure, are not transferable to a machine to make a new version of a human. Currently, a human can benefit from mechanical and intelligent limbs if any are missing (a Robocop sort of scenario), which differs from the so-called post-biological humans. We are more than learning, memories and the ego. My regret is that I did not refer to the Other of the body for the subject on that occasion with the AI specialist. This chapter seeks to articulate and atone for what I failed to say then.

Psychoanalysis and singularity

The fact that human-looking sentient robots might enter our eco-system is one thing, but transcendence of a human to another form of body is something else. Psychoanalytically, we could wonder about why someone might want to go beyond what is offered as a limitation to her/himself; living in a mortal body and dealing with a constant double-knowledge of knowing one will die one day whilst also keeping this fact as distant as possible. Jouissance belongs to the subject of body and language with a transgressive, transcending and destructive essence. Human beings have always wanted to traverse the limits of pleasure, as Freud pinpointed in his "Three essays on sexuality" and in his monograph "Beyond the pleasure principle" (Freud, 1905, 1920). What distinguishes the human subject from all other animals is not the instincts but the drives. The clearest example of this difference is in human sexuality. That is exactly why Lacan spent so much time unpacking the matter and finally arrived at the sexual non-rapport (Lacan, 1969–70). He gave the example of stickleback mating behaviour which, unlike the human subject's sexuality, is goal driven and seasonal (Lacan, 1953–4).

What my scientist friend seemed to be dismissive about was that the concepts "desire" and "drive" belong to the realm of a subject which has a subversive nature not exclusively owing to her/his intelligence compared to all other animals. Although Freud, in his "Three essays on sexuality", had defined the concept of drive as being directed at an object, Lacanian understanding of the drive's direction and topological movement gave it another form. Lacanian drive doesn't have a head or a tail; it is a surreal art of the subject, a "montage" (Lacan, 1963–64b). If, for Freud, reaching the object makes the subject feel a blast, Lacan suggests that the drive is not goal oriented as such; it circles around the object. The drive originates from the so-called erogenous zones, which are the lips, anus, ears and eyes (Lacan, 1963–4b).

One could wonder here how a sentient robot would be able to form parts of its body as erogenous. This differs from sensory learning and imitation. The AI can deceive humans but not have agency as a subject. It can generate a feeling accordingly but will not be able to gain pleasure from the drive. As much as psychoanalysis can be dismissive about some other sciences, the scientists seem to have limited knowledge of what constitutes a subject who develops desire and drive and has access to jouissance which is not simply a pleasure. Pleasure has a purpose and a goal: the relation between hunger and food, for example. It gets fully satisfied when it reaches the real object. If an AI is able to intellectually trick another AI or a human being, the drive, according to Lacan, plays another type of trick which is beyond the realm of intellect. The subject's drive tricks (a *tour*) the Real of sexuality and enables the subject to enjoy her/his flesh and blood body as much as possible. Excess and repetition belong to the realm of human drives. The drive, according to Lacan, has an aim which is to circulate around the object causing desire. Despite Freud's reasoning about partial drives, Lacan believed that drives are partial because they represent sexuality only partially (Lacan, 1963–4b).

While Freud thought that the drives are primordial and exist in the very nature of each human being, the Lacanian subject has an agency in forming and enjoying his montage of the drive. This has a pivotal role in many post-Freudian interpretations in the clinic of neurosis. However, Lacan in his eleventh seminar, returns to reading the Freudian drive and, unlike him, argues that the drive cannot be sublimated but desire can. It has a tendency to repeat and exceed, hence "all drives are death drive" (Lacan, 1964a, p. 848). Where Lacan does agree with Freud is regarding the four components of the drive: 1) motor force 2) the impulse (tendency to discharge), 3) and 4) the clear start and ending points (Lacan, 1963–4b). If Freud believed in so called developmental stages for the drives – oral and anal in polymorphous perversity – Lacan added two further drives to this list: the scopic and invocatory drives. The four drives in Lacanian theory do not follow the rule of stages as they do in Freud's conceptualisation of the oral, anal and phallic/sexual stages of the drive.

The Lacanian drive cannot be repressed. It is, in fact, the subject's ticket to remaining able to enjoy herself/himself as an exchange for becoming civilised and the sacrifice he makes at the level of jouissance right after his birth. From polymorphous perversity to an adolescent or an adult, the status of drives will remain the same. For Lacan, the subject's demands are linked with oral and anal drives while the invocatory and scopic drives as are related to the concept of desire. They are not the same concept but closely linked to each other (Lacan, 1963–4b).

One way to distinguish the two concepts from each other would be by referring to an infant who initially has to work out his need and survival with demand for an unbarred Other, the Real Other. However, as soon as language arrives, the subject forms his desire in relation to a lack, a barred Other's lack. As a result of the signifier of the Other's desire, the subject is barred (Fink, 1997).

In a documentary on singularity and AI, a sentient robot is brought to therapy for a sort of talking cure. The approach of the treatment – of what sort of neurosis! – was to explore memories so as to perhaps free the robot patient from the nuisance of an unpleasant past. A "past" had been programmed into it. This type of approach to human suffering does not include only AI; a flesh and blood human is believed to be cured if he un-represses the repressed in some kinds of therapy. The aim of doing analysis, however, is to enable the subject to gain an enjoyment, as much as possible, from his drives' arrangement, perhaps less troubling than before starting an analysis. In other words, the drive won't be rectified in analysis. The "rectification of the Real" (Lacan, 1966b, p. 601) involves a change in a subjective position towards the limitation of his fantasies and the brilliance of the object in order to find out about his own true desire. Eventually, the subject allows herself/himself to enjoy the jouissance of her/his drives, a little more relaxed than he was before entering into his journey of analysis. The drive cannot be reduced to the signifier. As such, the drive is an "exit only door" for a subject, from a trouble which is brought upon him by the "pleasure principle". To clarify this a bit more, I shall give you a clinical example.

An analysand came to see me a few years ago searching for a possible answer to the question of whether or not to have a child. She was 37 years old at the time and had a limited number of eggs, reducing the chance of pregnancy. She spoke of her own mother and her constant complaints about having children. Apparently, the mother had a total intolerance towards her children making noises or speaking loudly. However, the analysand was a constant talker, "a loud speaker" in her own words. She brought up a scene in her childhood where she had stopped her brother from crying by putting her hands on his mouth so tightly that for a moment she had thought that he was dead. From that moment on, she never stopped making noise herself and never stopped her other siblings from making a noise either. The effect of her guilt was to refuse to be dead or to deaden, refusing to comply with her mother's wishes. She also noticed in the work that this pattern had reached her adult life too; she is herself a big noise-maker. She was a successful musician and was always quiet in any social context. I just pinpointed the object of the drive – the noise/voice – not emphasising any other elements in her story. She then talked about her miserable childhood, miserable due to a lack of verbal communication with her mother, and the signifier "not being heard" came up. She realised that she wanted a child of her own with whom to create a relationship/verbal communication. She wanted to making noises: her music. Her desire was to make good noises. My intervention aimed at a libidinally charged signifier, which had marked her. She accepted a promotion in her work which involved travelling to another country and having a better position as a musician, in this case as a composer. She made a choice. She didn't want to have a child and seemed to have a less troubling relation to her "drive montage" at the end of that year.

The AI scientist whom I mentioned earlier, spoke about modes of survival and how humans wanted more and better. I do not intend to dispute this. However, transgression more than survival would be at stake when it comes to reflecting on the motivation behind wanting to create a "post-biological" human. The subject wishes to traverse and transgress. This is beyond a simple survival mode which the subject shares with other species. The drive should be distinguished from instinct based on the fact that the drive has a constancy not a rhythm (Lacan, 1963–4b). One can say "No!" to a dessert after a meal just as one cannot have the same food every day. It is not a matter of need, hunger or fullness. There is no such thing as a satisfying food for a human. Do we have anorexia and binging or bulimia in animals exactly in the same way that we have in a human subject? I am convinced that we do not see orthorexia in animals. Refusing to eat and being "empty" (of food) can be more satisfying for a patient with an eating problem. The enjoyment attained from the scopic drive changes a subject's way of dealing with hunger. Humans have certain rituals for reading, studying and sleeping etc., which cannot be maintained all the time. We tend to be punctual but cannot help becoming bored with chores and rituals from time to time. The drive does not understand rules, punctuality, rationale. It is not clear when exactly a drive's circulation has started and if it is supposed to end.

"Can an AI become a pervert?" This is a question I asked my AI specialist friend. His interpretation of perversion was rather different from a psychoanalytical understanding of the term. The drive is not perverse as some believe. A voyeur looks at what exactly? He searches for the lost object of the scopic drive, which is the gaze. He looks for a literal object, the one which cannot be seen, as if he truly wants to see its absence. Is it possible to see an emptiness? He keeps watching the scene desperately nevertheless. According to Sergio Benvenuto, the pervert has a double-knowledge regarding his mode of enjoyment through the process of disavowal. A voyeur assumes that he is included in the sexual scene yet his disavowed knowledge is that he is not (Benvenuto, 2016).

The solution employed by an exhibitionist is to make himself the object of the scopic drive: the gaze. He is the victim who is looked at. The pervert assumes that he is the object of the Other's enjoyment while he knows that he is not. A perverse act of eating faeces can be interpreted as the subject's refusal to accept the fact that a drive doesn't have an object. He fills this lack with a real object. In fetishism, the real organ does not represent the phallus. Phallus is a signifier, which is actually empty of any jouissance. A fetishist is the literal phallus (penis) of the mOther with which she is assumed to get satisfied. Again, he knows that she does not have a penis but he has disavowed such a knowledge. If the direction of a treatment in the clinic of a neurotic subject is hoping to get the Other to a barred O, the pervert believes in the barred Other right from the beginning. For a Don Juan, everyone is crack-able. He is "the phallus" for women, and not simply searching for a mother figure in the many different women whom he seduces. That would perhaps be a psychotic solution to work between the Real and the Imaginary but a Don Juan position does not have a psychotic structure. AI does not have agency to disavow a knowledge and then to deal with a double knowledge.

Wanting to create an eternally alive human being with all the correct intentions behind it is indeed a perverse position. It is believed that every aspect of a human being is transferable to the machine, including the concept of the unconscious which some scientists think they have gained a true understanding of. Well, if a bunch of repressed memories, or perhaps the effect of sociocultural discourse on the human psyche, is all that is meant when we refer to "the unconscious," then yes, everything is transferable.

The AI revolution has already started and seems unstoppable and inevitable because it originates from a very strong desire. No matter how much a subject might deny, resist or dispute it, s/he wants it to happen. Even though many argue that the arrival of the AI era would create a dreadful uncertainty, wanting to access an excess is the very essence of a subject.

Drive is not an entity which can be learned, modified or included in the realm of intellectual knowledge. Nor can it be consigned to the realm of sensation and feelings as it was in *Ex Machina*. The specialist wanted to do a final test on an AI with the help of an IT programmer. He invited the programmer to share his feelings when interacting with a female shaped AI – instead of using his intellect. For the programmer, the gaze and voice of AVA, the female-looking AI, which are a human subject's properties, touched him. It was not simply his so-called insecurity, which had prevented him from having a relationship with a woman up until then. The manifestation of a desire and the arrangement of the drive in a subject is beyond the rules and laws to be learned about dating and seducing another human.

Conclusion

To sum up this chapter on the drive, I wish to refer back to an old story. I think that I should acknowledge it now that I am secretly a luddite who denies it from time to time.

This is a brief account of the *One Thousand and One Nights*:

A king apparently had a beloved wife who betrayed him and started a love affair. The king found out about the affair and killed both his wife and her lover. As a result, he lost his trust in women but not his sexual appetite; he decided to have sex with a virgin every single night, killing her at dawn. He had already killed one thousand women when Shahrzad, the daughter of the king's minister, put herself forward. She was the one thousand and first in a row of virgins. As her last wish before sleeping with the king, she demanded that he allow her to tell a story to her sister. While she was recounting the story to her sister, the king was eagerly listening. This lasted until the dawn. She did not finish her story – obviously – and the king decided to wait for the second night so as to listen to the end of her story. Shahrzad also played her feminine tricks here: she told her sister the most exciting story and, of course, a slightly longer one! A ground-breaking start. Putting the question of feminine jouissance aside on this occasion, I shall only focus on the acts of storytelling and of listening attentively. Telling a story so as not to reach the final verdict: death. Storytelling every night for one thousand and one nights was not, perhaps, a better substitute for her capital punishment. We can assume here that she was perhaps secretly interested in a game of seduction.

What seems to be often overlooked in the story is the King's act of avid listening until dawn for one thousand and one nights. Not sleeping for almost three years! What a successful plot for a Netflix series. Well, her stories were good certainly, but more than her words, the signifiers, the coherence and continuity of the plot, with amazing cuts at dawn, that was her "voice", her highly addictive voice.

In an analytic setting, things happen in reverse to Shahrzad's story – except in some rare cases when the analysand starts an analysis with rage against the analyst. In the beginning of the *One Thousand and One Nights* story, there was not love but the question of death. Then, it leads to love; she makes the king fall in love with her. It is said that a love was born thanks to the contents of her exciting stories; Shahrzad unravels the king's heart from hate, anger and a grudge through her stories. There was a trick to play there. However, the king was enjoying himself at the level of his drive and was hooked by exercising and experiencing the ecstasy offered to him via his invocatory drive. He was listening to a gripping voice: the object of the invocatory drive. Well, sometimes they must have had sex too, as they had three children after one thousand and one nights.

There is always a look, a voice, a smell which stimulates not only the so-called erogenous zones, the sources of the drive, but also sets off a turmoil of excitement: a *tour* (trick), which goes around and around, a-temporal and truly eternal in the way in which no AI can ever be.

Bibliography

Benvenuto, S. (2016). *What Are Perversions?* London: Karnac.

Fink, B. (1997). *A Clinical Introduction to Lacanian Psychoanalysis*. Cambridge, MA & London: Harvard.

Freud, S. (1905). Three essays on the theory of sexuality. In: J. Strachey, ed., *The Standard Edition of the Complete Psychological Works of Sigmund Freud, Vol. VII*, pp. 125–249. London: Vintage.

Freud, S. (1920). Beyond the pleasure principle. In: J. Strachey, ed., *The Standard Edition of the Complete Psychological Works of Sigmund Freud, Vol. XVIII*, pp. 7–64, 125–249. London: Vintage.

Lacan, J. (1953–4). *The Seminar of Jacque Lacan: Book1: Freud's paper on technique*. John Forrester (Trans). New York & London: Norton.

Lacan, J. (1963–4b). *The seminar of Jacque Lacan: Book XI: Four Fundamental Concepts of Psychoanalysis*. Alan Sheridan (Trans). New York & London: Norton.

Lacan, J. (1966a). *Écrits: Position de L'inconscient*, 1964a, pp. 828–850. Paris: Seuil.

Lacan, J. (1966b). *Écrits: La Direction de la cure et les Principes de son pouvoir*, 1958, pp. 585–646. Paris: Seuil.

Lacan, J. (1969–70). *Le séminaire XVII: L'envers de la psychanalyse*. J.-A. Miller (Ed). Paris: Seuil, 1991.

Chapter 7

Unlocking a door

The position of the analyst

A journey

When thinking of the above title, I realised how much I was being pulled back into the memories of many years ago, to a time when I could not imagine that I might one day be "formed" and thus able to take up the position of the analyst.

I was not sure from which angle to approach the question. It was one of those moments when one's mind is sharp and ready to get a job done in one go but then hesitation gets in the way. It seemed that my thoughts and theoretical knowledge were in an active mode and racing to be both "creative" and "productive". The knowledge of theories was more or less present but as soon as I wanted to start writing a sort of resistance set in.

So, I questioned this resistance. Nothing came of it until I realised that one cannot approach the notion of the position of the analyst from any other angle than being somehow situated in that position itself. The question needed to be elaborated at two levels: first, the process involved in the formation of the analyst; and secondly, the function of the analyst in that position.

Lacan was already an experienced clinician, trained as an analyst, and yet he had felt a lack in the way this position was interpreted and functioned. Before taking the question on board seriously, a specific moment needed to arrive. He gave the moment a momentum and voiced his discomfort with whatever was referred to as the role of the analyst in the transference. In other words, what led Lacan to propose a different position for the analyst was that many readers of Freud had misinterpreted his work on handling transference. It was the early 1960s and Lacan was expelled from the IPA.

One decade earlier, during the 1950s, Lacan had challenged the concept of "counter-transference" which had been developed in the object relations school. What would be the purpose of a treatment?

The trace of his objection to the so-called "position of the analyst" as the target of counter transference can be found earlier than his eleventh seminar. In both seminar 8 and 10 on Transference and Anguish, Lacan questions and disagrees with the role associated with such a position. In later years, he scrutinised this position in different ways.

Before any analyst positions herself/himself in an analytic relation, s/he has embarked upon a journey of formation. During this process, s/he seeks a sort of knowledge, motivating her/him to be trained and to return every time to her/his own analysis, one session after the other. It is easier to pinpoint the inflection point when an individual/patient, demanding a cure/answer – from the "subject supposed to know" – shifts to become an analysand than it is to pinpoint the shift from the state of being an analysand into that of the analyst.

To summarise, the huge efforts here involve the following: dealing with one's own demand and desire in relation to the Other, bearing anxiety in relation to the Other's desire, accepting the fall of many enjoyable fantasies and traversing the fundamental one – if there is one – to become able to deal with one's own lack as castration, as well as finding a way to enjoy, at the level of one's drive in relation to the Other of the body and language, understanding the symptom in an analytical framework and then striving to move towards the sinthome.

This is a hell of a long journey! Then one could ask why on earth would someone want to take up a position which involves a constant reminder of their own "désêtre", as Lacan said? There is definitely a jouissance which is specific to each analysand to be formed as an analyst. But the position of the analyst is not a masochistic position. Nor is it a sadistic position to want to keep another subject's division alive. What is it then?

I was trying to answer the above questions from a position, but I did not know from which one, until eventually the day arrived. I was driving on a country road one day in autumn. The context eventually put things into perspective for my chaotic and confused mind. This title was only approachable from the perspective of a journey, a process: of what we call a "formation process". This was also the case with the birth of the notion itself in Lacan's work. It did not appear in his work all of a sudden and also never ceased to evoke Lacan's attention here and there throughout his teaching of psychoanalysis. He travelled through the theory and practice of psychoanalysis, not being satisfied with what was offered as an ideal and prototype for this role.

My journey was at two levels.

At school

The years prior to my psychoanalytical training were all about positioning a position rather than forming a position. In other words, the boundary between wanting and being – not even becoming – a practitioner seemed to be clearer. One does not necessarily need to become a patient in order to be a better doctor. The start and the end of the journey between training/studying and then practising were clear.

The question of knowledge after taking up such a professional position was one of "top-up knowledge", thus making the professional more equipped for those unpredictable moments in the clinic. The so called "top-up knowledge" was gained based on statistics on new clinical cases with new manifestations of illness. The newly designed methods based on such knowledge were applicable to many similar cases with the same symptoms and signs.

At home

My grandmother had told me stories of becoming a medical practitioner, in all of which certain signifiers were repeated over and over again: health, care, patience, endeavour, intelligence and the stepladder! Every single time, I was accompanying her going up the staircase, or I was sent up the ladder to bring her a piece of old decoration from the attic, she gave me the analogy between education, learning and training to achieve a graduation and this mode of climbing. Once, as a young child, I asked her what would await me after I finished school. She replied, in her poetic language, that I would be dressed "in white". This was the reason for my irrational anger towards my very first analyst's intervention one day.

I had spent a night-shift in the surgery ward before having a session. I had rushed out of the hospital without changing my uniform. In her office, I realised that I was still in my white coat. I apologised to her for still being in my shift uniform. In response, she said: "analysts do not need to wear a white coat". I was angry and did not want to renounce the symbolic value of the "white" coat.

What was happening in my life back then? I was an angry doctor soon to become a surgery resident and knew how to position myself in relation to my symbolic lack. My relation to the signifier of this lack, the phallus, had found meaning in white/green/blue uniforms. In reply to my analyst's remark I said: "yeah, but surgeons have to."

Wondering, hesitation and questioning were always with me while functioning from a position of a medical doctor. A few years ago, when I lost my beloved grandmother just before a talk I was giving on "Psychoanalysis today", I decided to say something about her, and I found myself saying something about "feminine jouissance". This is another idea in Lacanian theory which is not far from the position of the analyst. Later in this chapter we shall see how they converge.

After saying a few words on the significance of her presence in my life, I wondered why I had not interpreted her statement on "wearing white" as, for example, a wedding dress? The two positions were polarised in my mind. However, I had made them both somehow appear. That is how I made my version of womanhood accessible.

What happened next? Fast forward a few years from that day in my first analyst's consulting room: an end-stage patient with a malignant melanoma pushed an act to emerge from a desire. Her words at her deathbed moved me: "living and surviving are too complicated for medicine to understand them". This time I felt anguish. Far from being angry, I was so alienated from my "subject supposed to know" position. A fantasy had eventually fallen and with that came a change in destiny.

Lacanian orientation

My own "position of the analyst" started from being the worst analysand. My learning from medical school and my reading of human suffering from all sorts of "scientific" angles were pushing me backwards. To be more precise, they were exteriorising me. The ignorance of knowledge was an obstacle to a real formation process. Now, looking back on the analytic setting which I had inhibited, it was rather a battlefield between two angry doctors. I was a stubborn analysand looking for another stepladder to climb, or a new form of existence to fall into. To become an analyst meant to identify with and be qualified like my analyst.

Back then, I did not know that Lacan, as early as the 1950s, had questioned and criticised the ego to ego relation between the analyst and the analysand (Lacan, 1953–4). The analyst's position was neither a blank screen nor a flat mirror. I was seeking a knowledge – but what knowledge? Certainly not of what I understand today as analytic discourse.

It would be helpful to take you back to the start of my journey as an analysand to consider this position, so as to make sense of the Lacanian understanding of the position of the analyst. Today, in my practice many analysands confirm to me what a terrible analysand I had been – at least for the first six–seven years of my analysis – when observing how some subjects are so advanced right from the start with regards to the way in which they relate to their unconscious dynamic.

Where do we position ourselves as analysts today in the analytic setting when we work with neurosis in the Lacanian orientation? What sort of knowledge do we deal with in each case?

I remember my own analyst handling my demand for an understandable knowledge, the knowledge which would allow for understanding the cause "cognitively". It took me years to distinguish my kitchen table coffee-cigarette debates with friends from going for analysis. A psychoanalyst colleague recounted to me his first encounter with his analyst in his youth. Apparently, he had asked a question on the theory of sexuality and in reply his Swiss analyst had said to him jokingly that they would have this type of conversation when he would turn 60 while smoking their pipes and having a drink. Now, it makes better sense to me why it was that I stopped taking my coffee cup to my analyst's consulting room as soon as I became an analysand embarking upon a formation process as an analyst.

It is not easy to approach this question by relying simply on available Lacanian theories on such a position. In fact, this is one of those subjects within psychoanalysis which requires a subjective position that cannot be explored objectively from the outside. The position of the analyst is not a target point to be arrived at and never functions in the same manner all the time in every case of analysis. What seems to distinguish all different schools of psychoanalysis from medical and many therapeutic approaches to human suffering is the question of qualification: the end of training and graduation. The "completion" of training in a psychoanalytic school goes beyond simply requiring a certain degree of knowledge and experience to become able to function from a particular position that is to cause and effect. Therefore, this does not prevent an analyst in the formation process from functioning from the position of the analyst. Psychoanalysis is concerned with the effect of the position rather than the qualification for such a position to be taken up at the end of a certain training. In other words, the position of the analyst is not simply equated with the end of the training process. The educational knowledge of the analyst does not guarantee his functional position as a causative object.

Lacan's trajectory of approaching the question of "the position of the analyst" starts with Hegelian thoughts on the Other's desire. Then, he opposes the idea of transference and the so-called counter-transference before his eleventh seminar in 1964. A few years later, on the effect of psychoanalytic training and the analyst of the school, we have "the proposition of 9 October 1967 on the psychoanalyst of the school". Eventually, he designed "the pass" – a process through which to find a way of understanding the position of the analyst. He never put forward a theory on the position of the analyst as what it *is*, but rather as what its *function* is. The analyst is (1) a subject who occupies such a position to (2) function at the level of (3) the Real unconscious.

Being an analyst is a permanent and full-time job, but only on paper! The job description involves a constant renewal in every clinical case. Case by case, the analyst's function and his codes of duty change. Her/his position is only metaphorically a pair of listening ears, sitting on a chair behind the couch. He is situated in the position of the analyst somewhere in the analytic discourse operating with the analysand in and from the realm of the unconscious. S/he operates from a position far from "knowing what s/he does" as s/he does not know beforehand and does not have any clue where to situate herself/himself as an operating agent before the start of each clinical case. After positioning oneself in the work, the mode of operation does not have any instruction or protocol. The analyst reinvents a mode of operation every single session, in-tune with the analysand's unconscious dynamic. They both operate beyond the chair and couch on "the language" beyond spoken words. The analyst's position does not have any pre-existence as such. Now, regarding the type of function we associate with the position of the analyst, Lacan described Socrates' and Plato's roles as the analyst and philosopher respectively. In Plato's "Symposium", Socrates questions certainty around truth and desire. He is not seduced by Alcibiades' efforts and offers. As early as Lacan's eighth seminar on "Transference", the analyst's position is equated with an "agalma holder" (Lacan, 1960–61). The analysand assigns certain qualities and characteristics to such a position, holding something which the analysand desires. In Lacan's teaching, the desire of the analyst evolves from the Other's desire to a desire of "désêtre" (Lacan, 1967). As such, the analyst does not merely function at the level of the symbolic law, the law of the father (Lacan, 1964a).

In Lacan's view, the analyst's position is beyond a phallic function. In other words, the analyst's desire does not function at the level of "secondary repression", which is only a metaphorical and symbolic function. Rather, the desire of the analyst targets primary repression, dividing the subject and his desire. It aims at desire of nothing, on what cannot be said or articulated (Lacan, 1966a). Lacan, in his four discourses, puts the position of the analyst at the level of the *semblant* of *objet a* as cause of desire (Lacan, 1969–70). This is an operation beyond the symbolic, coming from the void of what is lacking. Therefore, the position of the analyst is far from a puzzle-solver or indeed a truth or fortune teller. The analyst in the Lacanian orientation distances herself/himself from the position of the "subject supposed to know".

The function of the analyst depends on the way in which he relates to his own desire as a subject, but his desire in the work is not defined as the desire of the Other. The analyst has rather an artist's position in relation to what is alien to the analysand. The analyst reshuffles the symptom from which the analysand complains to give way to the construction of the analysand's sinthome. Lacan brings a new light to the position of the analyst in Seminar 17, *The Other Side of Psychoanalysis*, in challenging Freud's Oedipal myth. He de-phallicises the concept of the desire of the analyst. According to him, the function of the analyst goes beyond the function of the dead father. The analyst's desire as a subject differs from the desire of the analyst, while occupying that position in the clinical work (Lacan, 1969–70).

Each analyst develops his own version of its function in a specific mode of practice. To follow Freud and Lacan is not the aim of being formed as an analyst. Searching for the validity of their theories in each clinical work would be equivalent to "not doing" an analysis. It would be merely the analyst's own sinthome with little or no effect on the analysand, to construct a way in which he can then deal with his mode of being.

If for Freud the position of the analyst means accepting the loss of the object and castration, which he equated with the feminine position in relation to the phallus, then for Lacan the function of such a position is to ensure the radical mode of not being he called "désêtre". Each analyst finds his own "exit-door" through which to form the position of being a cause through his formation process as an analyst. When Lacan formulated the position of the analyst as the place for causing the analysand's desire, he distanced such a function from being only interpretative of unconscious fantasies. If the analyst frustrates demand in order to allow desire to burgeon and articulate itself, this does not reduce his position to target only desire. In Lacan's later teaching, one could see his emphasis on the "destitution" for the subject as an exchange of a "restitution" – as might be the case in other therapeutic approaches. However, there will definitely be a way for each subject of analysis to deal with and enjoy her/his being. The analyst's desire is not confined only to the analysand's well-being. As a result of this desire, the analysand finds her/his version of compromise in dealing with his "non-being" in a certain way.

Here, I would like to refer to a rather common belief amongst some analysts that women make better analysts. This is only true if by "being a woman", we are evoking a non-existing position of *The woman* in both male and female analysts. The position of the analyst needs to function from a non-existing position like "The woman", which operates not only on phallic jouissance but on the "Other jouissance". As there is not a universal form and symbolic position of "The woman", we cannot simply set a qualification point for "becoming an analyst". In other words, the closest analogy to the position of the analyst in Lacanian theories is "to be The woman". Being attentive to something beyond phallic jouissance, that is, to the Other jouissance as is also the case with the position of the analyst.

To sum up, the position of the analyst moves from "subject supposed to know" to "being cause of desire" and eventually operates at the level of original repression and Real castration. The desire of the analyst is targeting a very opaque mode of jouissance which cannot be addressed in any form of symbolic register. In the next part, we will explore the clinical implication of the analyst's position in today's practice of psychoanalysis.

Clinical implication of the theory of "the position of the analyst"

In today's clinic, what is one doing in – and from – the position of the analyst when there is such a huge market with all sorts of promises for reaching and keeping one's well-being? How could one choose from such a broad range of approaches to one's own suffering? Not only do many not know what they have chosen as a therapeutic approach, but many who *do* know what they have chosen chose psychoanalysis to seek a consultation for a problem, but do not seem to know what they have really signed up for. When someone hears that through some approach he will rediscover his happiness before the end of a season, or that he will start from "A" and will end at his desired "B point", the comparison with the popular conception of psychoanalytic "promise" is stark. It is frequently said in pop culture that psychoanalysis is an open-ended process, that nobody knows where and when it ends, and that the ending is not necessarily a happy one, if indeed there is an end at all. Additionally, one may hear that on seeking help from one's analyst s/he may keep dismissing your demands and frustrate you – "you should find your way out of the problem yourself". With this stark contrast in mind, why on earth would the person in question choose the psychoanalytic approach to tackle their issue? It is indeed a bad marketing strategy for the work of analysis!

Beyond all of these misrepresentations, those who have experienced psycho-analysis know very well that going beyond the ordinary "bla-bla" of everyday life is enjoyable and that the result of doing analysis will accommodate their expectation of finding calm and relief from whatever they used to complain about in the beginning. Living a life without any guarantor gives a subject more autonomy in making choices for her/his mode of living even if making choices remains generally difficult both before and after analysis. Gradually, through psychoanalysis, what orients a subject in life becomes more or less clear to her/him. This makes the analysand a desiring yet divided subject, enjoying her/his division. However, one thing is certain: this state will not be achievable without accepting a challenging process. The analyst helps a subject, who complains about her/his symptom, to become an analysand during preliminary sessions and gives her/him a chance to open a door to an "unknown". To bear not-knowing and confusion would not be possible without collaboration between the two, the analyst and the analysand, at the level of the unconscious.

Lacan challenged and reinvented Freud's work of psychoanalysis. This is why the process of psychoanalysis became much longer than Freud had suggested and hoped for. It is an open-ended process with many possible exit-doors. Hence, it is terminable and yes, there will be a way for each subject to be eventually satisfied with her/his chosen mode of being, her/his own artwork.

These reworks are not a recommended method for practitioners to use or apply in their clinical works. There is a subjective construction in relation to the analytical framework in the Lacanian orientation. I would like to turn here to some of the challenges with which psychoanalysis is faced in this day and age. More than a century after Freud started his journey of discovery, what place does it occupy now in today's culture of quick production–satisfaction? This question needs close attention and much more elaboration. Here, I would like to reverse the question from "why psychoanalysis as a treatment for a potential analysand/explorer?" to "why become formed as an analyst and choose one school of psychoanalysis over any other?"

Of course, this is not the same question for everyone as each analyst/subject has a different stance towards it. As I mentioned earlier, the position of the analyst in so many ways is not as easy or as desirable as one might think. This question became even more confusing for myself precisely when I wanted to choose which kind of psychoanalytic training to embark upon. The choice seemed rather more complicated than moving from surgery to psychoanalysis. I found a way to solve the issue relying on the clinical aspect of psychoanalysis: both my personal analysis as well as my own clinical practice.

An obstacle was felt both at the level of theory and practice. Lacanian notions were too challenging to grasp and to employ in practice. I had faced certain questions that my first training in a non-Lacanian orientation was not able to answer. I was not yet convinced to start another training. So, how did I make up my mind?

What struck me about the Lacanian tradition was the approach to making a diagnosis. It was the structural clinical approach to the subject's suffering. The effect of the treatment with a new compass was also very different to my previous clinical experience. I approached Lacan from a critical position. I still do, but for a different reason and from a different angle. The new orientation had moved my position as analyst in the work with different psychical structures. Next was the question of handling transference and interpretation. I was not comfortable with some of Freud's approaches to interpretation in his clinical cases as well as with the post-Freudian way of handling the transference.

It seems to me more or less clear now that I would have left psychoanalysis as a way of treatment sooner or later if I had not come across the Lacanian clinical style of questioning. The position of the analyst is not a philosophical position, although it does contain a philosophy within it. It is not a position of a teacher or a mentor. Yet, it allows you to take up such positions – if necessary – in relation to some clinical cases. It also gives you a compass which nevertheless does not decide your mode of practice.

A reminder

The position of the analyst which we have discussed so far involves occupying a position in relation to a neurotic structure. In my clinical experience, more than any other encounters, the style and effect of working with psychotic structures changed due to the fact that Lacan had elaborated on psychosis beyond both the psychiatric clinical approach and the Freudian way of understanding them. I will give you an example of working with a case of a paranoiac subject who had been given a label of "obsessive compulsive disorder". Without going into great detail, I shall present a clinical vignette of the case of this young man.

He was tormenting himself and his partner with repetitive persecutory thoughts. He was manifesting cleaning obsessions as well. Classical attempts – ranging from medication to all sorts of therapies – had failed him. One particular intervention had even worsened his condition. Apparently, one therapist had encouraged him to do further investigations to make sure of the validity of his delusional persecutory thoughts. Another had taken up a position of a catholic priest, a passive listener to his detailed account of his activities every single session.

The whole of each session was filled exclusively with his speech about the persecutor, and nothing else. Classical approaches had little effect on enabling the paranoiac subject to close off the rupture of the Real from which he was in great pain. He was suffering from the excessive jouissance of being in these persecutory thoughts. In the Lacanian framework he was helped to organise his thoughts and find an exit from the Other's constant intrusion. The position of the analyst in this case of psychosis did not function as cause of desire. It did not function solely as a reassuring agent either. In many cases of patients with psychotic structure, the analytical framework in this orientation helps the subject to organise and construct a solution with which s/he deals with the foreclosure of the Symbolic order.

Working analytically with psychosis is not about an emphasis on the division of the subject and her/his desire, as in neurosis, and nor is it just about pacifying an eruption in the register of meaning – schizophrenia – or the intrusion of the Other – paranoia – nor simply obstructing the self-reproach mechanism by encouraging the subject to have fun in life – melancholia (Leader, 2011).

Interventions on spatial and temporal metrics have a significant function in this framework to reduce the excess of jouissance in mania and the lack of any purpose in life in the severe low phase seen in manic-depressive cases. You see how the position of the analyst differs in relation to clinical cases of psychosis. The work would not happen without the system of structural diagnosis.

It is a common belief that Lacanian clinical practice is equal to short sessions and theatrical interpretation. If we take the position of the analyst as a function operating beyond meaning (the Imaginary) and the Symbolic, the analyst might wish to use any possible way to avoid closing off the unconscious dynamic. Many analysands have experienced the momentary block in the flow of their speech in an analytic session. For an analyst, this point is taken seriously by not simply reducing it to, for example, the unconscious resistance in transference. The time of the unconscious is not tuned to our usual way of understanding linear time. Besides, what is aimed at in psychoanalysis is what is most alien to the subject: what cannot be articulated, or is articulated but not heard. If we push this a bit further, the role of the analyst is to enable their analysand to get rid of the semblances/metaphors of the spoken words/signifiers to unveil the object cause of desire (*objet a*). If, for Freud, the ultimate goal of doing analysis was to come to terms with symbolic castration and the phallus was the target signifier to work through, in contrast, Lacan developed his ideas in terms of the function of the analyst and the Real castration which produces the *objet a* (Lacan, 1964a).

From a position of cause, an analyst enables the subject to produce master signifiers and find a way to cope with his original division. As Lacan states, the drive has a supplementary function for a divided subject. Finding a way to enjoy at the level of one's drive would not be achievable if the analyst gives his own version of a repair to the subject.

An analyst in training, besides learning from his own unconscious, before finding his mode of practice, gradually discovers first when and from where *not* to intervene. Many start to practise relying on their own analyst's style. It takes a bit of time for each analyst to form his position in each clinical case, developing a unique way of working with the unconscious. However, the position from which an analytic act takes place is the same for all analysts. Only the modes of conduct, technique and strategies will differ. The aim of interpretation from the position of the analyst, again, would be the same for all analysts. There are many means of interpretation besides the analyst's few words here and there. Interpretation operates beyond the semblance of language and traverses the law of the symbolic. Some analysts use theatrical interpretations as well as silence.

At the level of the Real of the analysand's desire and drive, the analyst's desire finds its meaning. The analyst as a subject does not operate from her/his subjective position in the work, and does not wait for a manifest-ation of one's true desire to then move on to the montage of the drive. As mentioned earlier, in analysis the Real unconscious is neither mathematically logical nor linear. As such, the knowledge of theory plays a minimal and limited role in an analytic setting. Many analysts have other careers before or besides their practice. In other positions in everyday life, the question of knowledge and technique matters in a clear way. In psychoanalysis, how-ever, these elements are put into question. The love of knowing is replaced with a strong desire to bear confusion while exploring the unknown: the most alienating knowledge.

The analyst punctuates the analysand's discourse to break the habit of repeti-tion of a daily rhythm. At this point, an analyst's function is similar to that of a music arranger. When a shift in the subject's discourse takes place, both the analyst and analysand become researchers, with a specific research method which does not involve the discovery of *a* truth. They work together from, as Lacan said, two different positions: the analyst in the place of the agent puts the analysand's unconscious in the place of the Other to work (the analytic discourse).

Yet a clinical case is not equivalent to a research project for the analyst to conduct an investigation on the analysand. "What is a clinical case?" is an important question for all clinicians working in the field. Each clinical case is rather a source of learning. That which is learned is the way in which each analysand deals with her/his unconscious desires and his arrangement of the drive. The analyst's knowledge of the analysand's unconscious is not devel-oped any further than the analysand's; he has, however, used his mode of lis-tening to the unconscious, which is very different from the usual habit of listening to ordinary everyday discourse. If an analyst sees all the cases pre-sented to him as "a case presentation", he will not be able to listen and follow the logic of the unconscious dynamic at play.

Freud is the best example of both being and not being a clinical researcher. He was a true researcher when he raised questions about what was not simply explained by available investigative methods into human suffering at the time. He also manifested his confusion, blindness and ignorance about the clinic of neurosis and psychosis. However, occasionally, after elaborating his theoret-ical formulae, he tended to be more dismissive about what could have been found at the momentary opening up of the unconscious, which is considered as "what cannot be said", by over emphasising the meaning of symptomatic manifestations.

The analysand is to produce a master signifier, which repeats itself under so many different semblances. It is not heard, or is heard and taken for granted. From the production of the master signifier (S1), a sort of knowledge in the place of truth is gained. The analysand knows somehow what to do with this truth at the end of analysis. Along the way, the analyst pushes the subject of analysis to question what he takes as a given fact (Lacan, 1969–70).

Without wanting to oversimplify Lacanian concepts, one possible analogy between the two positions of the analyst and the analysand which are not equivalent to two "minds" in the analytic relation, as the dynamic of the unconscious from both sides is at play, would be that of a music arranger and a composer respectively. The music is already made when it is handed to the arranger. Everything is already there in the discourse when an individual arrives at the analyst's consulting room. Psychoanalysis is not merely an excavation and discovery of what is dumped in the unconscious in an archaic form. It also contains invention. It is a constructive process putting the subject into the work so as to bring her/him eventually to a "testimonial" state.

This process cannot be carried out, like the music arranger's task, without listening to the different sounds of the written notes of each single instrument: "the Letter". An analyst designs a specific style to let the subject's personal montage of the drive become manifested and then to discover an enjoyment from the arrangement that is different and less painful. The position of the analyst is crucial in that it prevents an analyst's act from closing off the unconscious, as Lacan said. This was exactly what motivated him to revisit this position at the level of both theory and practice. The key to the door of going beyond this risks turning into a lock on the door, and the opportunity then being taken away from a subject who desires and deserves so much more than a treatment voucher.

> *"To the memory of my grandmother who was most*
> *patient to my nonsense and to my very loud rock, metal music!"*

Bibliography

Lacan, J. (1953–4). *The Seminar of Jacque Lacan: Book1: Freud's Paper on Technique.* John Forrester (Trans). New York & London: Norton.

Lacan, J. (1960–61). *Le Séminaire Livre VIII: Le Transfert.* Paris: Seuil.

Lacan, J. (1963–4b). *The Seminar of Jacque Lacan: Book XI: Four Fundamental Concepts of Psychoanalysis.* Alan Sheridan (Trans). New York & London: Norton.

Lacan, J. (1966a). *Écrits: Du « Trieb » de Freud et du désir du Psychoanalyste, 1964a,* pp. 851–854. Paris: Seuil.

Lacan, J. (1966b). *Écrits: La Science et La Vérité, 1966,* pp. 855 877. Paris: Seuil.

Lacan, J. (1967). La Proposition du 9 octobre 1967 sur le psychanalyste de l'École. pp. 14–30, In: *Scilicet 1,* 1968.

Lacan, J. (1969–70). *Le séminaire XVII: L'envers de la psychanalyse.* J.-A. Miller (Ed). Paris: Seuil, 1991.

Leader, D. (2011). *What is Madness?* London: Hamish Hamilton.

Chapter 8

Having a breakdown on the motorway

Supervision

The beginning

I was driving back home, listening to Yasmin Levy's album, *La Juderia*. A late October evening on a busy motorway, her heavenly, deep voice keeping me in a trance. A long blast of the horn from an impatient driver burst my mood. I had passed my exit: an exit that, to me, promised rescue from the long queues of traffic jams. It was a sharp turn-off, leading to the place I called "home, sweet home"! The time Yasmin's deep, emotional voice entered into the world coincides with the time I started my journey of formation in analysis. I had passed my exit – my last gateway back to feelings of familiarity and comfort – to become almost lost on a never-ending motorway. At the time, the end of that motorway was under construction, as was my confused mind. The music was not helping me concentrate on finding my way back home either, as if it was inviting me to remain lost in the mood. There was no way back, and I think that I was actually enjoying it. Then, just as I was beginning to search for a corner to pull over, to stop myself from pursuing the journey, I had a breakdown on the motorway and my vehicle could not go any further.

Earlier that evening, I had all my thoughts focused and clear in order to discuss a patient's case with a supervising analyst, for the first time outside the psychiatric ward. He was facilitating a private supervision group for the few clinicians who provided the "talking cure" rather than solely prescribing drugs for them. No exit pass, no bad driving habits: I was confident in my diagnosis and knew how to present my case to the group. It is indeed easy to speculate that what I had confronted in that supervision meeting had distracted me so much from my usual, clear pathway. I was going to "supervision", but I only just realised and registered the meaning of this on my way back home.

Throughout my clinical training, prior to my analytical formation, the meaning of this term "supervision" did not have such significance in terms of its implication and its function in the clinic. It was, rather, more or less equivalent to appointing someone who had superiority and maturity in carrying out a technique or transmitting knowledge. It was somehow literally having a "super-wiser", with a super/mega vision of what we were doing in the clinic. One could carry out clinical work under instruction of a mentor-like professor. It is no wonder that the first few generations of psychoanalysts, who were mainly medical practitioners, had invented all sorts of supervision-related theories, in all of which the pattern of a transmittable set of theoretical and practical methods seemed to be both possible and necessary.

Studying some historical cases of psychoanalysis, it is indeed striking to find out that this approach to the question of training and supervision has not itself been questioned – or, even worse, has been copied, though we know that working in such a way has little or adverse effect in the clinic. The question of supervision and clinical training has always been a political question, something that has to do with the politics of psychoanalysis. Wouldn't it be easier if Freud had had something decisive to say on the topic? He does not have any theories on this which seems to have led, to a certain extent, to some confusion around the "mode of practice" with the concept of "supervision". The first generation of psychoanalysts, such as Sandor Ferenczi and Helene Deutsch, tried to conceptualise a theory of supervision. Ferenczi's approach, for example, was to discuss a clinical case with a colleague, while Deutsch tried theorising the question of supervision and training. Her suggestion was to have a patient seen by a supervisor as well as the trainee analyst (Deutsch, 1935). The so-called "Deutsch style" was still in use when I started my analytical training under a group of psychoanalysts, and it made me question the place of the supervisor in clinical work.

Introduction

The 2016 movie *Dr Strange* is about the case of an arrogant neurosurgeon who loses the ability to use his hands while conducting surgery. In the search for a solution – to get him back on track – he ends up consulting a seemingly spiritualist mentor called "the Ancient One". In the scene of their first encounter, there was not a single word which this maverick doctor said that I was not in agreement with. His belief in science as a guarantor against ignorance and superstition meant his argument with the Ancient One initially took the right approach – until he says that he can "see through" anyone, including the Ancient One. This is the moment that he is made to question his certainty and trust in given facts. Although I did not agree with a single word of the Ancient One's dialogue in that particular scene, I approved of her approach to the "all-knowing" position which seeks to provide the single solution. Poor Dr Strange! His state of absolute shock over what had happened to him, or, perhaps, over something having surpassed his unquestionable abilities, reminded me of myself many years ago.

Now, by the start of my second analytical training, I had learned my lesson in terms of how to seek knowledge when in the clinic with patients suffering from either their symptoms, modes of being or excessive jouissance. I was also well acquainted by now with a different style of supervision, which was far more cynical towards the idea of shedding light on a fact in order to bring out a piece of unconscious knowledge. However, Dr Strange's moment of shock in the movie resonated with what I felt after leaving my second supervisor's consulting room in the middle of a chilly day in late summer in London. I was truly doubting *everything*. Worrying thoughts of all kinds were rushing at me – from "Am I myself mad or not?" to "Have I done something harmful to the patient?" – and generating enormous anxiety in me. As I walked up a hill, I began to feel that I had perhaps wasted all those years since I began my journey towards formation. However, in the next few years, it was proved to me that I was wrong in that conclusion.

The main shift in my training cannot really be pinned down to a precise moment during my supervision or personal analysis; my position in clinical work was re-questioned and worked through again and again. This was a dramatic change in the way in which I originally perceived the concept of supervision in psychoanalysis; what was important was not the style but rather what was at stake for a supervisee to look for, in the clinic. It became hard to differentiate between an analytical session and a supervision.

History revisited

The history of supervision in analytical training involved a means of ensuring "authenticity" within a practice which had been taking place since 1925. The IPA Congress in Bad Homburg, Germany, was the starting point for establishing a set of standards for psychoanalytical training, and hence the need for supervision as part of the pathway to qualification (Safouan, 1995). As a new concept, it was treated as an institution from the first; it became an integral part of training and has been so ever since.

The ITC (International Training Commission) was for 15 years chaired by Max Eitingon who had a clinic providing both therapeutic services and the training now considered as the inception of training standardisation (Moncayo, 2008). Before then, the supervision dynamic was far less formal. Two peers would share their thoughts, findings, dilemmas and wonderings about a clinical case. Regardless of how effective or restrictive this model of supervision was, it served the analysts of the time well. It also seems to be somehow closer to what we understand today, through Lacan's teachings, of the desire of the analyst and of the place of knowledge in clinical supervision compared to many other schools of analytical or therapeutic thoughts.

Freud had started with Breuer as his mentor-teacher, before moving to Fliess as his confidante–colleague, to address something of his patients' cases (Safouan, 1995). Until, eventually, he named one of his first patients as his great teacher. His desire for knowledge was continually redirected; from gaining knowledge from a mentor, to gaining knowledge from a peer, then from the clinic itself. He ultimately made his bet on the subject's repressed unconscious in order to get to "a" knowledge. Furthermore, the agency of each clinical case taught him how to approach the unconscious. Obviously, as he himself did not go into analysis and did not experience the effect of supervision, he was not pushed beyond where he felt his limits to be.

Before the 1920s, there was no such a thing as a systematic, institutionalised psychoanalysis. However, soon after this time, the idea of becoming a psychoanalyst became associated with being supervised often by at least two supervisors, while still placing emphasis on the analyst's "skill" within their career of psychoanalysis rather than discussing the position of the analyst in the work. It is still a common belief of analysts to think that discussing a case in their personal analysis would help them to become a more expert or mature clinician, by detecting their so-called "mistakes" or "shortcomings". In today's way of thinking about being supervised as an analyst, discussing a case in either analysis or supervision is interpreted as finding out about one's own desire in the work: the desire of the analyst, which, according to Lacan, is a desire to analyse (Lacan, 1963–4). It would certainly not be correcting the supervisee's technique; rather, it would enable her/his competence in analysing the unconscious knowledge of her/his analysand.

The supervisor's role is an "enabling role" in many different ways. When we listen to a patient's speech, regardless of her/his psychical structure, what is communicated during the sessions needs to be taken beyond face value, beyond meaning. This involves a specific mode of listening, which is the endpoint of supervision in analytical training. How this aim is to be pursued in supervision depends on the ability of the supervisor to intervene at the level of the supervisee's desire to analyse. The supervisor's technique and mode of intervention are supposed to be in accordance with the supervisee's desire. A supervisee's creativity to conduct an analytical act is nurtured in supervision. Therefore, a supervisor within the supervision space does not occupy a teaching position and nor are they supposed to treat the symptom in the clinical case. This leaves the responsibility of analysis entirely to the supervisee.

Such an idea was explored in detail in a 1963 paper by Daryl Debell, called "Treat or Teach?" (Debell, 1963). The context in which this paper was written was a time in which the emphasis of training was focused on the concept of so-called "counter-transference". The trainee analysts in supervision were invited to reflect upon their own feelings towards the patients. Needless to say, this incorrect focus in supervision reduced the analytical framework to a mind spa for the supervisee! As a result of such an approach, the work was faced with a limit in the form of unconscious resistance. At this time – and still in some approaches today – patients were targeted "objectively" rather than being treated as subjects. The supervisee was encouraged to focus only on her/his own ego and learning process, making use of the work with the patient to do this. In fact, they were pushed to keep the work between two egos, when all they needed to do was distinguish their own from their patients'.

The demand for detailed records of patients' narratives in some approaches shows a strong tendency towards making the clinic of psychoanalysis an evidence-based, scientific practice. There is little questioning of the implications such recordings have, in terms of their function and effect on the direction of treatment. Speech is reduced to and treated only as a vehicle leading to the meaning of repressed materials. Bearing this in mind, it is no wonder that many clinical cases either stagnate or are broken off prematurely. Both supervisor and supervisee, in fact, are supposed to be detectives of ignorance. They look for what is said but not heard within the most primitive aspects of speech.

Setting many rather rigid standards to control the clinic is an obsessional strategy for tempering the analyst's anxiety in the work. The mentor or teacher whose role is to transmit knowledge or correct/modify a trainee analyst's mode of practice (similarly to the medical training model) acts in accordance with the structure of law and regulation referred to in master or university discourses rather than being concerned with each subject's circumstances, as in the discourse of the analyst (Lacan, 1969–70).

In contrast to the usual belief that institutional regulations serve to save and guarantee the quality of training for a member of the public, right from the outset they actually ignore both supervisor and supervisee's ethical positions in relation to a subject. The position necessary to truly guarantee that each clinical case is treated ethically requires a radical disbelief in the "all-knowing" position.

In another vignette from *Dr Strange*, Strange himself tries to behave in relation to a master: a man who sits behind a desk, making Strange believe that he (the man) is the Ancient One. The way Strange was brought up within a grand, hierarchical institution of academic knowledge has taught him little of how to live life without such guarantors; he is surprised to see that he is actually served a tea by the Ancient One herself. All his learned standards evaporate in the face of a different kind of power, and he no longer needs surface appearances to prove his abilities to others. Throughout the plot, we see his unknowingness put into play. He has to unlearn the knowledge he has striven to learn. As an overqualified doctor, the qualities he learned were his allies in becoming a competent healer of the human body. After he realises his ignorance, he becomes more and more able to devise and master his own mode of conduct. The Ancient One and her crew made him come face-to-face with his ignorance, rather than allowing him to remain entangled in his illusions. He lets go of his understanding of given facts. Through his new training, he is strongly advised against copying or identifying with the master. He is pushed to question even his mentor in order to defend his own case. He is faced with more danger whenever he gets close to copying another mentor's position. He has to form and (more importantly) claim such a position for himself, which he eventually does. He understands such a position only when he gets there and knows how to treat it.

Such a model of supervision, which sits outside the standardisation of medical and health-related practices, reminds us of a dynamic in the Socrates–Alcibiades relationship. In Plato's symposium, which Lacan referred to throughout his eighth seminar, *Transference*, the mode of clinical training (of which a part would involve supervision) is depicted well in Socrates' approach to the question of teaching and mentoring while still maintaining the role of nurturing a follower's ability to question, rather than being focused simply on handling the transference (Lacan, 1960–1).

There is certainly a question of knowledge and experience involved in becoming a supervising analyst. However, what this "knowledge" and "experience" might be needs to be expanded upon here.

Why supervision?

From Helene Deutsch's calling supervision "controlled analysis" (Deutsch, 1935), to Lacan's choice to term it "pure analysis", the desire for knowledge changes in meaning and function when occupied within the position of a clinical supervisor. Both the above types of approach towards supervision, however, show the need to be aware of such a position in the formation of the analyst: the analyst who forms the desire to make sure that the clinical work does not serve the purposes of the analyst's enjoyment of given knowledge in a case, as well as the enjoyment obtained from knowing her/his own symptom – as the latter gets in the way of the direction of treatment. The desire to know reduces the function of the analyst to an agent of the inquisition – much closer to a perverse position – and gets in the way of analysis, as Lacan had pinpointed throughout his teachings.

The supervisory role is to protect the direction of treatment from being diverted, a diversion from the desire to know about one's symptom in order to create a specific way to treat it. In a supervision session, a supervisee might present a case when things have already gone wrong in the work. The first, fundamental rule is to avoid taking the position of a "fixer". Instead of treating the case presented as a patient being handed over, the role of the supervisor focuses on searching for "why" and "at what point" the work had seemingly stagnated, encountered a resistance, bungled actions or even an acting-out. Such a goal cannot be obtained if the supervisor in question – for whatever reason – is searching for the answers outside the realm of the unconscious.

When a supervisee seeks a supervisor's view on a clinical case – most likely in order to double-check something – there could be a chance to elaborate on a symptom in the supervisee's own analysis. It would be colluding with the analyst's symptom if the supervisor does not suggest this to the trainee analyst. Then, it would be the analyst's responsibility to work through such an intervention by the supervisor. Such an approach in supervision does not mean that a supervisor functions in the same way as an analyst regarding the supervisee's unconscious material and desire. On the contrary, a supervisor pushes a candidate in clinical training to recognise the whys and wherefores of becoming an analyst. In other words, her/his desire to analyse is helped to burgeon and is nurtured. The place of knowledge, what is interpreted and why, are the real questions to be raised in the supervision.

What is supervised?

This question opens a path to work through after there is a demand for supervision in the first place. Treating such a demand could potentially be a good start to punctuate the dynamic of a supervision session, as a way to enable a supervisee to get to her/his desire for doing analysis. In other words, how the supervision is to be used by the supervisee, and what is the aim in seeking another analyst's intervention, are the two main questions to be worked on as soon as a supervisor is appointed. When someone wishes to polish her/his skill in a specific field of expertise, the contract between the supervisor and supervisee is quite clear, and the question of change and modification is also kept at the level of learning and knowledge. However, the question of change in the work of analysis is supposed to happen at the level of the subject, which has surprising effects.

A while ago, a supervisee – a counsellor – doing his psychotherapeutic training outside the Lacanian orientation, consulted me about "repairing the patient's aggressive transference" further to an interpretation he had made to his patient. Apparently, he had been anxious about losing the patient prematurely, so he had tried inviting the patient to talk about why he disliked his therapist, putting the focus of the work between the two parties into an Imaginary register. In the supervision, he was again putting the emphasis on his own feelings towards the patient, which were caused by the negative transference. I interrupted him at that point, showing my indifference towards what he seemed to have paid too much attention to – both in the therapeutic session and in the supervision – and asked more about the patient's symptom and the implication of his interpretation regarding that specific material. Such an intervention in the supervision not only "surprisingly" brought up a significant piece of the patient's early childhood history – which had been totally neglected in the work up until then – but also made the supervisee question his type of approach to treating his patient. He was so concentrated on his own discomfort that he was not able to listen, hence he kept the direction of treatment circulating around his own anxiety, and made little attempt to question it. This was then worked through both in his analysis and in the supervision independently, but in the same fashion. He became more able to see the relation between his mode of intervention – at that particular moment in the work – and his own symptom. He was no longer trying to reduce the subject's desire to a demand and the focus of the work bypassed the realm of two egos. Something changed in the clinic as soon as his position in the work was shifted to take a rather more ethical position.

Supervision today

The focus of many contemporary approaches to the concept of supervision oscillates between either exploring the so-called "counter-transference" of the therapist/analyst, in order to make sure that a clinical practice is "pure" enough from any personal input of the therapist; or to transmitting a piece of knowledge and expertise. On the other hand, more emphasis is put on recounting the recorded narrative of a patient, leaving little space to question the implication and function of such recordings in the treatment. This understanding of the space of supervision in the clinic of psychoanalysis and psychotherapy reminds us of Lawrence Kubie's strategy in the 1960s: to keep all speech recorded, under the illusion of capturing speech fully (Kubie, 1958). It also reminds us of a trend that started in the 1920s when the institutional politics of psychoanalysis began to come into focus. Establishing certain rules and regulations, under the motto of "public protection" against malpractice, sounds like a benevolent idea. However, such an approach brings up a more fundamental question: protecting what against what?

Before Lacan's famous proposition in 1967, the "the proposition of 9 October 1967 on the psychoanalyst of the school", which shows his stance towards the politics of psychoanalytical training, little attempt seems to have been made to elaborate the function of such a practice, at the level of the subject and her/his desire to become an analyst (Lacan, 1967). Supervision alongside personal analysis is already given an essential space in the training – in fact, being supervised as a trainee analyst is a *sine qua non* of training. According to this proposition, the question of self-authorisation – which can sometimes be misunderstood and misinterpreted – brings the position of the analyst into something beyond being the "subject supposed to know". The analyst is a "destitute" subject, whose desire concerns only analysing. This proposition indicates that a supervisor supervises the framework of a clinic to make sure that such a position is in place for a supervisee who is in the process of formation. In other words, a supervisor oversees how the analyst is acting, from a non-existent position beyond a dogmatic knowledge of theory. Moreover, the narcissism of the analyst's ego, which can keep the demand of an analysis at the level of just demand instead of elevating it to a desire, is the target of a supervisor's intervention. An analyst is supposed to get satisfaction from doing analysis, and this would certainly not happen if the actions of the analyst come from an "all-knowing" place. An "expert" supervisor encourages such a desire to operate beyond the demand for a cure from a symptom. Such an intervention from a supervisor would not be possible if s/he tends to be only the provider of a certain "supposed knowledge" about the case.

Therefore, what is "overseen" in supervision is ensuring that the supervisee analyst is the analyst of the work, and certainly not someone who entertains himself with the "meaning" of the material. The purpose of a functional supervision is to bring the Real out of the material provided: to keep the direction of treatment from stagnating, of being diverted, and from being fooled by the mirage of knowledge which will only give a "temporary fix". The subject will certainly acquire knowledge from her/his own symptom throughout an analysis – leading to a sinthome formation – but this differs from a knowledge coming from the Other. In other words, an analyst's work is under a supervisor's audition – Lacan used the term "super-audition" instead of "supervision" in 1975 – to generate an effect on sinthome-formation, meaning that the supervisee does not occupy the position of the Other in their work (Lacan, 1975).

According to the above, the framework of analysis and supervision are similar in terms of their aim and function. Both a supervisor and an analyst operate from the place of producing a desire. A desire to search for – and hopefully find out about – the "not-yet known" material within the unconscious. Mustafa Safouan proposes that supervision is a process of "apprendre à apprendre", meaning "learning to learn".

Going back to the question of "public protection", when a practising psychoanalyst is pushed this far to go through a journey of "destitution" to restore a new subjectivity, and when her desire for analysis is put to all possible challenges, from personal analysis to supervision, which push her more and more to question the place of knowledge in the work, which institutionalised law of the state can possibly operate ethically in relation to this? Furthermore, it would be the patient/analysand – at the front line – to realise and judge a clinical work when there is, for example, an issue of malpractice. Within such a view of the supervision and psychoanalytical training, searching for a "guarantor", for an Other controller – which is antithetical to analysis – would be unnecessary. The "destitute" subject of the analyst is the strictest critic of her/his own work.

Perhaps it would be helpful to mention at this point too that supervising a case – while having structural diagnosis in mind – raises a question regarding how the different clinical structures would be supervised. Do they differ from each other in terms of how the supervising analyst operates from the position of "causing a desire"?

When a clinical case is presented to a supervisor, as we mentioned earlier, the reason for the request for supervision needs to be explored. Similar to the analytic setting, a period called "preliminary sessions", which can last much longer than one might imagine, would be needed. The purpose of preliminary sessions – apart from gathering some general, given facts and materials about the patient's past history and symptomology – would be to punctuate the narrative in order to get to the most basic properties of the language used, where a sort of truth lies – in both senses! Therefore, the main question to be formulated is: what is at stake in the supervision in this particular case? Through the preliminary meetings, a supervisee analyst finds her/his own way to formulate her/his question in a space of supervision that can sometimes be mistaken for her/his own personal analysis. This is a point to be emphasised for further elaboration in another space: one's personal analysis. Within the realm of the unconscious, from where the analyst's and the supervisor's interpretation comes, any trace of a desire or the resonance of a drive is "overseen". This makes the supervisee remain in the position of the analyst in the work. What mode of practice, how to interpret, or perhaps the style in which to conduct an analytical act, is not the focus of such a style of supervision. The point of a supervisor's actions is to nurture a stronger desire "not to know/understand", on the part of the supervisee. This could be when, for example, a demand to "Give me an answer" is put to the supervisor; or when such a demand, coming from a patient, receives too much of the supervisee's attention. In a way, a supervisor is supposed to be attentive at two levels: trying not to occupy the position of the "subject supposed to know", but rather that of an *agalma* holder. In such a way, a supervisee would allow herself/himself to meet and form her/his desire of doing analysis. As such, regardless of the question of diagnosis, the position of the supervisor remains the same. Clarifying a diagnosis with a supervisor would be again in accordance with how to orient one's work to keep the direction of the treatment in place.

Conclusion

Supervision is more than a political theme in psychoanalysis and it should be part of the ethics of psychoanalysis. Theorising such a concept in Lacan's teaching is at the heart of the analyst's desire. This shows how such a concept needs to be approached and treated. The idea of setting standards becomes absurd due to the fact that the position of how and when to form them is within the power of the subject. Many people ask when does a psychoanalyst start practising as a supervising analyst? As soon as s/he is appointed by a supervisee of the school and s/he agrees to be a "super-audition" of a clinical case. There is no finishing line for learning to learn.

Many years have passed since my first encounter with a supervisor's act at the level of my desire: many years since that breakdown, an emergency stop, which I am most grateful for, a breakdown which marks the beginning of my never-ending journey. From a shocking encounter, to an anxious walk after leaving my second supervisor's room; it was quite a longish, rocky path to walk. Now, off the couch, sitting with my coffee next to the window, a supervisee continues: "I guess this is a question for my analysis!"

Bibliography

Debell, D. (1963). A critical digest of the literature on psychoanalytic supervision. *Journal of the American Psychoanalytic Association*, 11: 546–575.

Deutsch, H. (1935). Control analysis. In: *The Therapeutic Process, The Self and Female Psychology*. P. Roazen (Ed.). Eric Mosbacher (Trans). pp. 239–246. London: Routledge, 2017.

Kubie, L. (1958). Research into the process of supervision in psychoanalysis. *Psychoanalytic Quarterly*, 27: 226–236.

Lacan, J. (1960–1). *Le Séminaire Livre VIII: Le Transfert*. Paris: Seuil.

Lacan, J. (1963–4). *The Seminar of Jacque Lacan: Book XI: Four Fundamental Concepts of Psychoanalysis*. Alan Sheridan (Trans). New York & London: Norton.

Lacan, J. (1967). La Proposition du 9 octobre 1967 sur le psychanalyste de l'École. *Scilicet*, 1, 1968: pp. 14–30.

Lacan, J. (1969–70). *Le séminaire XVII: L'envers de la psychanalyse*. J.-A. Miller (Ed). Paris: Seuil, 1991.

Lacan, J. (1975). Conférences et entretiens dans des universités nord-américaines. In: *Scilicet No 6/7*. J. Lacan (Ed.). p. 42. Paris: Seuil, 1976.

Moncayo, R. (2008). *Evolving Lacanian Perspectives for Clinical Psychoanalysis*. New York: Routledge, 2018.

Safouan, M. (1995). *MALAISE DANS LA PSYCHANALYSE. Le tiers dans l'institution et l'analyse de contrôle*. P. Julien, M. Safouan, and C. Hoffmann (Eds.). Paris: Les Cahiers d'Arcanes.

Chapter 9

A resident of the world

Forgetting the past

The question of "history" will be approached from two different perspectives in this chapter: *History* as every individual's description of their life, and history as the history of the parlêtre (Lacan, 1975–6). The former concerns any individual(s) in singular or collective form, while the latter focuses on the particularity of each subject's self-created history.

History includes all biographies as well as autobiographies, looking through the lenses of the apparent reality of events and occurrences and the repetition of these events in a cyclical format. Time within *History* is mathematically linear and the impact of socio-political events on collective and individuals' lives is included in it. However, in *subjective history*, the question of the eventuality of impact is seen from a different angle. This angle takes into consideration the subject's choice. The subject chooses to put happenings into perspective according to a certain subjective arrangement: in this respect, *subjective history* is a testimony. The spatial and temporal elements do not follow the rules of physics. In fact, *subjective history* finds meaning in topology. It ignores the laws of predictability and it is differentiated from what is perceived as cyclical repetition in *History*. The two conceptions of history outlined above follow trajectories which run in parallel yet are not fully independent of one another. There will be points of convergence – points from which the subject forms her/his testimony. Partly as a result of *History*'s impacts, the subject tells her/his version of their story/history.

History is concerned with the past and with time that is passing. The eventuality of the future is considered based on the patterns in the past. Here, the question of choice becomes a limited one due to the fact that there is a dyadic and linear relation between cause and effect. An incident is or is not likely to happen depending upon past experiences. The probabilities are much discussed and negotiated once we face the question of the past, present and future in the realm of *History*. Monuments, artworks, museums, history books and novels are all attempts at not forgetting, of remembering or of preserving the past, with little attempt to answer the question of why the past should not be forgotten, or how it is remembered.

For many, the Channel sea and its cliffs can be a reminder of a historical event at Dunkirk: the evacuation which took place in 1940. Meanwhile for a particular subject it could be a reminder of a much earlier event in childhood, such as the experience of overwhelming anticipation as she awaits her/his rescuers. In the latter, the impact of the event is registered as an invisible mark. It is this invisible mark with which psychoanalysis is concerned. In psychoanalysis, we create a potential for every single individual to explore her/his *History* in order to create a *subjective history* beyond the story of her/his life or what is taken to be their destiny.

However, the parlêtre of our civilisation can never be independent of the Other: the Other of *History*, the effect of *History* on her/his living body. In other words, the Other of the body and language are inevitably affected by *History*.

The past

A while ago I re-experienced the mark of *History*'s effect, a reminder of what remains under one's skin, at an unexpected time. I was preparing for a talk at a conference on "The effects of contemporary socio-political events on individuals' mental suffering" when I received a phone call from a solicitor working for one of the immigration offices, dealing with a never-ending application. Due to a minor typing error in my documents, a radical decision was made. Despite my certainty of "I am staying", an enforcement letter was due to take away all I had built up in the previous years. The solicitor was saying something on the phone which I could not register and cannot recall. I was absent from real-time and suspended from a subjective temporality. A "no matter what" decision was made. A file, a number, a label: you, one of thousands in the queue, were waiting for a decision to become de-suspended. I do not wish to go into the details of this challenging process and the suffering resulting from it. In the mode of suffering, the subject is and always will be alone.

It took me 19 days before I was able to put those few moments into words for the first time. Yet I did not feel successful enough in fully exhausting the meaning of what I really felt in that particular moment. I had survived the momentary suspension again. The outcome of my efforts to describe the feeling is as follows: in a frozen fraction of a second, when all the movements around you suddenly stop and you have a panoramic view and a clear sense, nothing seems to be registered. You struggle with a feeling of whether it is only you feeling what you are feeling. You are absent in your own presence. You push to return, to come out of the void. You first hear a constant ticking sound and the next thing that you hear is a banging noise exploding in your head. You are suspended from nowhere; suspension is the experience from which you want to survive. You make your choice and you are back: back to your usual senses and time resumes its passage.

Back to my senses, I realised that I was in the middle of writing a book and had a deadline with a publisher. I had my talk in a couple of weeks, which I could not possibly imagine cancelling. I had my notes prepared but they needed to be written as a paper if someone else was to volunteer to give the talk in my place. Above all, I had a line of patients arriving in less than an hour. It seemed that I had momentarily forgotten one aspect of *History* which does not include the subject. I was focused on what I was doing and I was aware of the paradox.

I took a cold shower and started my clinic. During the night, I re-drafted my talk as a paper to be read in my place by a colleague. I also noticed how my second language was escaping me all that day and for a good few days afterwards. The written works in my hands were in my mother tongue and had a great pacifying effect in those moments. I seemed to believe that I had fought and defeated all the suspensions in my life up until then. I had assumed that I would have become a survivor by doing so.

History is already there when an individual is born. Everybody in my generation was born into a discourse affected largely by big social events: revolution and war. Before my arrival on planet earth I had my first experience of suspension: my mother spent three days in labour. It was not safe to step outside. It was wartime. My mother feared for her life, that she may lose it, and I was fearing to have it. Life seemed to be too much of a responsibility to take on. Besides, this delay of birth had found an expression in my mother's narrative. She used to refer to the date of my birth and blame the prolonged labour for making me wait for another year to start a primary school. Schools in Iran used to start on the first day of autumn and my date of birth meant that I had to wait until the following year to start school. My symptom of being in rush to finish and graduate from school originated from her equivocal expression of "being late".

For many years, I avoided speaking about many unusual experiences in my life: from revolution to war, from surviving a terrorist attack to immigration and exile. I did not want to escape the reality of the past, of *History*, I was very conscious of not reducing suffering to certain "buzzwords". I wanted to preserve this suffering from the Other's enjoyment. The suffering in and from the past had a priceless value. I was adamant to keep it subjective; a private matter to be used in a way so that the Other's unnecessary intrusion is bypassed. When a much earlier event leaves an irreversible mark on you, you become wary. A second chance would not be your first thought before making a choice. Besides, surviving becomes a mode of being. The past, however, gets revisited.

After the 1979 Revolution in Iran, suppression in every sense of the word was brought upon the country. Culture, more than anything else, became the target of the attack. Everything was turned upside down overnight. My generation's *subjective history* is intertwined with *History* of major social suppression as well as war. The sound of a passing train or the noise of the fireworks on New Year's Eve were felt differently in later years as a result. The subject of analysis becomes able to enjoy travelling by train and watching spectacular fireworks over the Thames but, still, a suffering is recalled.

What happens outside a family can play a fundamental role in affecting a family discourse. It cannot be detached or avoided. *Subjective history* does not function totally independently from *History*, as we have said. No matter how much parents tried to protect the new generation of infants from the war by keeping the rituals of everyday life in place – closing the curtains, playing loud happy music to muffle the sounds of bombardment – the war was felt out there from every possible angle. Schools were closed and children were home-taught. The anxiety of the mother was felt in her palpitations and the way her made-up smile was undone. All the made-up arrangements of ordinary life would function as semblances, with pacifying effects on the children of the war. However, the invisible impact was still active in leaving its mark.

Neverland

In my *subjective history*, more than any other element in my life, the land beneath my feet has been highly valued as much as it has been transitional. Many of us enjoy moving, a symptom generating a mode of jouissance for each subject in a particular way for a particular reason. It gives a sense of freedom to many. If the element of freedom is stripped away from the concept, it takes a very different turn: one becomes an exile, entangling the subject in a closed circuit. The subject would not be able to go back to where she has started her journey as a point of reference: her home. Those who have experienced an earthquake know very well that more than being concerned about something falling from above, it is the shaking ground beneath one which generates a horrifying sense of instability, an overwhelming sensation of anguish.

From and through *History*, I had learnt not to take the ground under my feet for granted, to the extent that this uncertainty became a mode of being. From an individual to a psychoanalytic subject, I eventually found a way to create a sinthome out of moving, out of the symptom (Lacan, 1975–6). However, you remain conscious of the shaky ground beneath. You will be reminded, long before your interaction with any immigration offices or borders. Every single time you hear about a war somewhere in this world, every single time you hear about an incident in Calais or Dunkirk, at the asylum seekers' camps, you are catapulted into both *History* and your *subjective history*. We have not reached a full century after the Dunkirk evacuation, nor the Nazi concentration camps, and yet today we hear about "the jungle", a name given to the camps at Dunkirk and Calais by Syrian refugees. It has never been a question of iden-tification with the people there for me, as I do not share the same or a similar experience in the past. A decision is made by a group of individuals who cause disasters which could have been prevented, as is the case with any major social changes such as revolution and war.

It is true that an oeuvre comes from a suffering. The trauma of the recent history of the twentieth century, the first and second world wars, left marks on the formation and on the continuity of psychoanalysis from Freud to Lacan. The major contributions of the Jewish community to science and to new fields of research, such as cybernetics, in the wake of the Holocaust are undeniable. In the face of major social trauma and suppression, of any intense kind, each subject will deal with it differently. However, the suffering resulting from massive social disasters can also cause turmoil and unnecessary regression rather than nurturing the subject's creativity. It can produce a perverted power structure, which interrupts the exploration of the unknown. It suppresses art and inflicts a survival mode instead of developing and encouraging new work. In such circumstances, what can one do and how can one deal with one's suffering, with one's symptom? *Savoir-y-faire* would not be the first priority of a subject whose primary concern is simply to survive everyday life (Lacan, 1975–6). Survival mode goes against any form of constructive development.

In the earlier vignette of my experience of suspension, a decision-maker had, again, shaken the ground beneath me. It was an unnecessary interruption which reduced, once again, *subjective history* to *History*, which was written on a piece of paper: a descriptive identity. It felt like an alienation. On paper, you are reminded of a past which you have gone beyond. This question becomes more urgent when the law treats certain identity papers differently. The identity paper which decided the fate of a young Syrian boy, Alan Kurdi, in September 2015 did not involve a subjective choice. He was a 3-year-old Syrian boy with a Kurdish ethnic background. His family had fled the Syrian war and tried to reach Europe amid the European refugee crisis. Alan, his family and many others decided to flee. He was drowned along with his 5-year-old brother and his mother. The war had led his family to try to obtain entry to Canada. Apart from the father of the family, none of them survived the dangerous sea. The war and the decision of some politicians in power repeated a past which could have been avoided.

From the Holocaust to Islamic radicalism, from war to terrorism, from racism to xenophobia, *History* affects *subjective history*. Personal choices – coming from somewhere beyond cognition or the ego – individuality and the opportunities to nurture humanity will be washed away from contemporary history when the past is forgotten.

Dunkirk: the shore of anticipation

In the light of both history and psychoanalysis, I would like to evoke *Dunkirk*, a movie by Christopher Nolan with a score by composer, Hans Zimmer, whose music in this movie inspired and helped me to write down what I could not talk about for a long time.

The Dunkirk evacuation could not be imagined or narrated subjectively any better than it was in this blockbuster movie. The narrative followed three strands, putting the individual in the position of a subject in the mode of "suspension" and "survival". Nolan pinpoints the "difficult choices" and "paradoxes" brought upon a subject by their situation (Nolan, 2017). Using visual and sound effects, the sense of unpredictability in such conditions is transmitted to the audience. The narratives are stripped from the plot, allowing the emotional effect of the art to transcend the rationality of the intellect.

The plot focuses on the subject's momentary choices and responsibilities, which are brought upon her/him. *History*, as described earlier, involves a linear and mathematical duration of time. However, in Nolan's movie, the momentary nature of coming to a conclusion – the urgency to make a choice for a subject – is taken into consideration and depicted.

When I was researching the history of the Dunkirk evacuation and its aftermath, I found two differing approaches to the event from France and Britain. The touristic memorial sites in Dunkirk have brochures in both languages, in which, again, you find the traces of a duality towards *History*. The duality, however, serves the same purpose: to keep remembering the past. If one version of the story sees the whole event as a defeat and a retreat – as Churchill called it a "colossal military disaster" (Churchill, 1940) – the other version is the story of resistance. This illustrates again how the position of the subject matters when looking into a history.

This movie's particular perspective aims at the subject, regardless of nationality or language, which are key components of *History*. The difference is highlighted at the level of the subjective choices made in a battlefield, on the ground or in the sky. In the three parallel narratives, what is addressed is not the question of triumph or defeat. The effect of every individual's decision, from a military commander to an ordinary Dutch citizen longing to escape, causes the saving or the loss of lives. Another example is the fisherman with a sailing boat who must decide whether to go ahead with his own plan or to stop and rescue a drowning pilot. In the face of the Real of the event, where all the political and military strategies seem to have collapsed, a civilian sailor decides not to seek safety: "there is no hiding from this, son." The law of wartime, would condemn him due to having disobeyed the rules, yet he transgressed and chose to follow his own interpretation. "There is no hiding from this" also echoes the moment of conclusion which each subject comes to in the course of analysis marked by an urgency.

In this movie, Dunkirk with its 400,000 trapped men, became an event in *History*, involving the *subjective* interpretation of the situations during wartime. Hence, the movement of the story takes us from a militarily disastrous defeat to the triumph of humanity.

To Shahbanu of Iran: The Empress of Art

Bibliography

Churchill, W. Speech 4 June 1940. Available at: http://audio.theguardian.tv/sys-audio/ Guardian/audio/2007/04/20/Churchill.mp3, accessed.

Lacan, J. (1975–6). *Le Séminaire Livre XXIII: Le Sinthome*. Paris: Seuil.

Nolan, C. Interview 18 July 2017. *The Guardian*. Available at: www.theguardian.com/film/ video/2017/jul/18/christopher-nolan-dunkirk-video-interview-harry-styles, accessed.

Chapter 10

From fury road to the awakening of the primal father

Introduction

How has the current political discourse created a space for radicalism and terrorism? What can we understand from the dreadful spectacle of our times, of increasing intolerance towards difference, when just a few decades ago we believed that we would all soon come together as citizens of the world?

The prejudices that caused the Second World War and the Cold War were never properly dealt with after those conflicts, a fact which ultimately led to the formation of religious fundamentalist groups and of their coming to power in 1979. This contagious radicalisation soon spread and is now a cancer eating into many parts of the world, affecting nations far beyond the borders of the lands where Paradise was once thought to be found.

The relationship of madness to decision-making in politics not only affects the life of the individual living under those regimes. It also leaves a broader, historical mark on social discourse in the longer term. The relationship between the discourse of the Other and the formation of the Symbolic unconscious is undeniable. How else can we interpret the lack of guilt felt around certain social and political horrors of the last century?

A radical belief in a certain ideology can be found in each of the psychical structures. However, each of them is associated with a different, underlying question. A psychotic subject might find his radical belief as a defence against constant doubting in the register of meaning (schizophrenia) or it might be a solution for a melancholic to reduce a torturous guilt. A radical faith in an ideology in paranoia can act as a mission to pursue in life in order to fight against an intrusive Other or delusional thoughts. Hence, radicalisation in cases of psychosis can be a solution to protect one's mode of being against going mad. Here, we could think of a "radical belief" as a sinthome which protects a subjective knot of being from unravelling. The fourth ring in the Borromean knot, which Lacan conceptualised in the Joyce case, keeps the subject's being coherent and protects him from madness.

This is not, however, the case with radicalised neurotics. A radical belief in a certain ideology can be a neurotic subject's symptom which translates the unconscious letter to jouissance in the Real for him. Each subject has an agency to form a symptom. According to the later Lacan's work on *symptom*, the core of a symptom originates, in fact, from maternal jouissance (mother tongue) and then it is the paternal metaphor which finalises its formation. The signification which is the result of a subjective interpretation of the signifiers in his mother tongue creates the core of a symptom. Then, it is the function of the paternal metaphor which has the final touch on symptom formation. A symptom's role is to separate a subject from the mother while helping him to keep going in life. A subject would be able to get separated from maternal jouissance if a symptom is formed. Otherwise, he will remain stuck in such jouissance. Through analysis, the status of symptom can be challenged or changed (to a sinthome) if it causes a great deal of malaise for a subject. In other words, when a symptom fails to deliver a tolerable jouissance for a subject, a change becomes necessary. Hence, in order to find some answers to the reason why a subject is radicalised, it would be essential to investigate the earliest life events and narratives in which each subject has lived through.

As we learn from the clinic of perversion, a pervert always wants to make sure that his perverse act would continue to serve him. For a perverse subject, the radicalisation of others potentially creates a symbolic structure which guarantees the possibility of continuing his perverse act. On the other hand, in the name of an ideology, what a perverse subject aims at is barring the Other. A perverse act generates a mode of jouissance for a pervert like a symptom does for a neurotic subject. Moreover, such a perverse act protects him against his overwhelming rage and anguish. To grasp fundamentalism or radicalisation in a certain ideology or religion, we need to go back to the earlier moments in the life in each person to find the trace of such signifiers at the level of both maternal jouissance and the paternal function. As we are familiar from the clinic of psychoanalysis, it sometimes takes a few generations for a family drama to become clear in this way, and it can manifest in a subject's symptom/sinthome or in his desire.

In recent memory, a psychotic solution – which I will explain more about it later in this chapter – to these questions has paved the way to the perversion of political power, both in the Middle East and in the States. Such a perverted power serves a purpose within a psychotic discourse. How would it be possible to tackle the issue and replace it with one that results in less conflictual and aggressive international relations?

Through the lens of psychoanalysis, we will raise some questions about social phenomena such as fundamentalism, radicalism and terrorism, reflect upon current social issues and question the approach of modern politicians towards both the formation of these expressions of madness and how they are handled.

History then and now

In the winter of 1979, in the main cemetery of the capital city of Iran, a crowd of people stood cheering for their angry leader who furiously condemned socalled "authoritarian political powers" inside the country and in the West. In his hate speech, one could hear the promise of excitement, epic change, holy salvation and even echoes of the ultimate battle between light and darkness. These were in fact only the sugar-coating for a wider trend that began to evidence itself soon afterwards, almost 40 years ago, a trend that ultimately led to the formation of a dreadful social phenomenon: fundamentalists' rise to power. A group – with a radical belief in religious laws coming from an Other sitting above all – with little or no tolerance towards difference. They had come together under one master signifier: that of eternal salvation – a false hope.

The capital of a country with thousands of years of history and culture, full of stories of resistance to some of the most violent invasions throughout human history, stood here reduced to empty gazes and a cemetery of bones. "God is great," a man screamed, and the crowd followed with the same refrain. There was no clapping as a sign of affirming the leader's inflammatory speech. Clapping was a sign of Western culture, which invaded religious beliefs! For many years to come, "God is great", replaced all shouts of celebration and the sounds of clapping hands. One can imagine what happened to music and dance, art and culture.

On that sunny midday in February, it was not only Persians that were stunned by the scene. The world's gaze was on that broad daylight Halloween. The corner of Paradise, the land of Shahrzad's *One Thousand and One Nights*, was to become an island of sighs and despair. In 1978, Rollof Beny, the late Canadian photographer, describes Iran in the record of his journey through the country "as old as history and as new as tomorrow". Less than a year later, a traditionally peace-making country – where many races and tribes with a variety of religious and cultural backgrounds had long since lived together with no big issues – was sending a clear message to the outside world that only this group of fundamentalists represented Iranians. It is indeed hard to believe now that they were ever given a space by both intellectuals inside Iran – mainly influenced by the Soviet Union at that time – and powerful politicians in the West, as an alternative power structure. The goal of the group's leaders and the true colours of their socio-political ideology only became clear to the Allies' wishful thinking after the fundamentalists had gained power and taken charge of foreign policy. The hostage crisis in the American Embassy, a permanent cut-off in relations with Israel, the support and encouragement of radical groups of Islamists around the world, from the Middle East to South America, and thousands of executions of leftists and communists inside the country, were all the fruits of that gathering in the cemetery, which was broadcast to the world as widely as it could be.

Their supreme leader said this in his first speech:

> Do not only be satisfied with the fulfilment of your essential needs, we will give you an ultimate form of spirituality. [...] The final victory will be with us as soon as all the evil hands of foreigners are cut off. We will make Iran great again under the shadow of Islam.
>
> (My translation from his Beheshte Zahra Speech, 1979)

His xenophobic and megalomaniac delusions of power, of being an incarnation of God, were bitter to some tastes but they were still very much palatable to others. Indeed, it still sends thrills down the spine of many people to hear this speech today.

Apocalyptic aspiration

In 2015, George Miller released the third instalment in his trilogy, *Mad Max*, which focused on contemporary narratives around the equality of men and women and, indeed, on modern feminism and female empowerment – beyond the phallic version of power – a power of adaptation and transformation, a power with no false hopes, a power originating from a free spirit. In the film, this is represented by the mother-women based on the other side of the desert – one could perhaps hear a touch of homophony between Lacanian *désêtre* (Lacan, 1967) and this group of desert women. On the other hand, there are also the women who are pinned down to milk machines, nourishing Immortan Joe, who drinks only milk and takes it in exchange for drinking water, of which he possesses all of the earth's resources. His power over water is his means to continue conducting his perverse acts. There are many ways to understand and interpret this great movie in terms of questions of power, madness and perversion. However, we shall focus here on the formation of fundamentalism as a perverse, libidinal economy trading on a psychotic discourse.

There is a female protagonist with a great dream, who takes with her the five wives of Immortan Joe, each of whom represents a different version of womanhood. Her hope for freedom – which comes from her fundamental fantasy – leads her to embark upon a jailbreak journey and she sets off to the Green Place, miles away from Joe's wasteland where difference is not tolerated. Under Joe's rule, female citizens are reduced to sexual objects or reproductive apparatuses. A clear-cut dichotomy between "us" and "them", and the homogenising dynamic of sameness within each separate side, tied them under the hegemony of Immortan Joe, who did not make the claim to be God, but rather used the signifier of God as a master signifier, which carried neither meaning nor libido, functioning to support his perverse mode of jouissance in dominating others (Lacan, 1963 4). Placing emphasis on hierarchical religious belief creates a symbolic system. Such a symbolic structure – a belief system – is always desirable in perversion as it creates a space for a perverse act (Benvenuto, 2016). What allows a perverted authoritarian system to enjoy its existence involves both barring and dividing the Other. Every Other can be made to crack, from a perverse perspective, and all one needs to do is find its weak point.

The question here would be: where is madness situated in such a dynamic? Throughout this surreal movie, which in fact is a reflection of many existing societies from our own time, we can plainly observe that there are followers of and believers in Immortan Joe, representing the primal father, who Freud referred to while elaborating on repression, guilt and the origin of religion

(Freud, 1913–1914). The primal father was a cruel figure who possessed all the women of the hypothetical tribe. His sons killed and devoured him. The guilt over his murder made the sons build and respect a totem as a substitute for the father. Our purpose here in referring to this Freudian term is not to follow his reasoning on the formation of neurotic repression, the return of the repressed, or on civilisation and its discontents. Fundamentalism is almost always associated with a group headed by a leader. Such a group's infrastructure is shaped by this top-down template. This sort of group structure can organise an excessive jouissance, which is not localised for the psychotic individual. What has failed to localise around the so-called erogenous zones during the early years of infancy and childhood will be focused on a radical belief later in life. The question of finding sameness and homogeneity inside a group is similarly a form of psychotic solution. One idealised image of power is taken to have all the answers and exalted as an all-knowing agency. Then, below that, the remainder of the small, elect group all remain equal – in the same rank – for the psychotic subject. This set-up enables her/him to remain in a sustainable relationship with the Other. When a symptom is not formed to separate a subject from maternal jouissance (Lacan, 1975–6) and the function of the paternal metaphor is foreclosed for the subject, a symbolic separation from the Other does not take place (Lacan, 1955–6). This never allows a psychotic subject to leave the nest. Xenophobia, rage and intolerance towards otherness can be part and parcel of being entangled in maternal equivocation which is found in the clinic of psychosis. The inclination towards an absolute, perverted power which seems to promise salvation from a chaotic interior, therefore, becomes a solution.

A psychotic discourse (an overemphasis on sameness) leads to the formation of a perverted, fundamentalist power. On the other hand, perverted power serves a purpose for the psychotic dilemma of being stuck in the limbo of meanings in the domain of language, which creates constant, torturing doubts about their mode of being and living (Lacan, 1955–6). The tendency towards black-and-white absolutism is often the psychotic solution to help the subject fight against the grey areas of doubt. Therefore, a radical belief in an ideology like this is an essential defence against doubt. On the other hand, responding to the demands of society with deliberately confusing false hopes can provoke the masses to revolt against such doctrines, seeking a substitute to reduce their alienating anxiety. The alternative would then be choosing the one who acts radically rather than only speaking of promises. Historically, the desire for radical change is almost always associated with a cry for a patriarchal substitute, preferably one with a "God" behind him, a God as a Real power supporting and guaranteeing the act of substitution that is taking place. The primal father is awakened!

In neurosis, "being protected" by a powerful figure is not simply a practical solution as it is in psychosis. In psychosis, another person's competence can compensate for the lack of confidence in a psychotic subject due to a failure in ego formation. A powerful figure to whom a psychotic subject confides can also be a solution (an Imaginary support) for dealing with an overwhelming jouissance both in his body and in his mind. In a neurotic structure, such a tendency has a different currency and hence functions differently. In neurosis, a desire for an absolutely powerful Other would be associated with a specific mode of jouissance beyond any Symbolic structure. It is linked to an idea that does not serve any practical function in the same way that we see that it does for a psychotic subject. Such a mode of jouissance is called Other jouissance in Lacanian terminology. This kind of jouissance is associated with the Other of the body as the first Other for each subject, while phallic jouissance is linked to the Other of language. In many cases of neurosis, we can find a fascination with a super powerful figure in life or even in fantastical stories. The bodily excitation felt by both neurotic and psychotic subjects upon encountering a supernatural power or horror is, in fact, an expression of such a form of jouissance in the Real body. In neurosis, the symptom of "being attracted to powerful figures" triggers Other jouissance in the Real body of a subject. The powerful figure triggers such an excitation in the Real body beyond the symbolisation of the body by language or beyond an Imaginary support of the body image. Living or working with a powerful Other in some neurotics is not simply due to an Imaginary identification or wanting to be protected against an imposing power. Why such a symptom is formed is the question we should elaborate at the level of a subjective interpretation of maternal equivocation in the early life for each subject.

We should be careful here not to generalise too much as we seek an explanation of such social phenomena from a psychoanalytic perspective. Understanding an individual's choice to adhere to a set of beliefs would require an understanding of a psychoanalytical interpretation of ethics, rather than of morality, which has more of an affinity with a perverse structure. Political correctness, the prejudice towards sameness and an inability to recognise difference, when united under the umbrella of morality, can ignite the fire of violence against otherness. This is due to the fact that a human subject essentially wants to be recognised among others and this is what happens through identification in the mirror phase, and through alienation and separation in the early years of life (Lacan, 1963–4). The Lacanian conceptualisation of the mirror phase which we explored earlier in "A black swan in the mirror" is the foundational theory of subject formation rather than of self or ego recognition. It refers to the infant's reflection in the mirror as the subject's first encounter with and realisation of her/his body as the first other, over which s/he gains mastery in the presence of the Other's – perhaps her parent's – gaze (Lacan, 1949).

Unlike Freud's ideas of group identification in his "Group Psychology" (Freud, 1920–1922), Lacan elaborates on the question of identity and group formation at the level of desire, the drive and ethics. There are groups – for example, psychoanalysts – in which falling-out and the rekindling of relations happens between members from time to time; there are also patriarchal groups – like the church – in which the group bond lasts for centuries. A patriarchal group's members share a homogenising sameness between them and become radicalised against the rest – everyone outside the group – at the level of the

Imaginary register. It should not be surprising, then, to observe that most radicalised suicide bombers come from a background of a minority group in which they have remained closed-off within a social structure that does not seem to accept or even acknowledge difference. The emphasis placed on integration, merging and adjusting to the new societies into which they have immigrated leaves limited space – if any – for the subject's liberation. Paranoia is part and parcel of such a group's formation. Even making a group the size of a nation does not change this structure – particularly in cosmopolitan countries.

Hope

Almost 40 years ago, Persian women and Persian culture – if the two can really be separated from one another – became the targets of a tyrannical totalitarianism that wanted them veiled to the greatest possible extent. Some Western politicians supported the change of regime, believing it would benefit the world in many ways. An "autocratic" system was replaced by a totalitarian regime that closed any doors through which to negotiate with the outside world. Inside, all was governed on a highly moral basis, on grounds that mainly targeted women. Any Western symbol represented a satanic element to be exterminated from social discourse. Moral force, as a perverse power, along with some elements borrowed from communism, restored the primal horde to dominance. Although over the decades the subversive subject was able to partially change the dynamic, the marks of such destruction on culture scarred the nation's symbolic unconscious, leaving a mark on its destiny.

One thing which needs to be taken on board here is the unpredictability at play within any human social network. Humans have historically always oscillated between states of lowering and raising of tension. No matter how much the propagandists do to tailor the people's expectations in accordance with a particular power structure, each subject is essentially subversive, and her/his acts are beyond the control of a structural morality. Any external attempt to predict the subject's actions will be complicated by the subject's ethics in relation to the law of jouissance and not the law of the state. Many interpreters, however, tend to dismiss this fact and instead become caught up in their fearful fantasies of apocalyptic destiny for nations. According to Lacan, the super-ego is not simply an internalisation of external prohibitions. The super-ego is an imperative agent which commands a subject to gain even more jouissance. As accessing a full jouissance is not tolerable for a speaking being, a limit which comes from a subject's ethics helps her to deal with the problematic of jouissance. Before a subject learns how to deal with the external law of social interactions, she has to deal with the law of both her Real body and the mother tongue. The subject has agency in dealing with an imposing law coming from the body and language. Hence, based on how a subject forms her knot of being, she decides how to relate the law of the state: when to obey or to transgress it.

To sum up, the way forward for our contemporary moment – a moment in which madness is the sanest version of survival – is located in the singularity of each individual subject's mode of being. Regardless of individual politicians' psychical structure, the psychotic politics of today are conducted so as to boost both rapidity of change and mass-production for constant consumption, a theme which would require an extensive elaboration on its own. The presence of unlimited options in any shape and form, and for any context, generates even more anxiety, which is difficult to accommodate on a large scale in society: this could also be a reason for the reawakening of the desire for a figure who is all-knowing and possesses the ability to give the subject answers and peace of mind.

When looking through the psychoanalytic lens, we do not entertain ideas of how individuals or groups behaving in a certain way can cause certain consequences for human society. We do not interpret an action in the world of politics from the angle of egalitarianism or authoritarianism. We understand that power exists beyond just the terms of phallic value. We are attentive to the particularity of each subject's desire in relation to the Other's power. Using preconceived knowledge in order to fix the issues – and offer a solution for the current situation in the political world – prejudices and blinkers the subject, unless, however, this knowledge comes from the true desire and power of will to make a change. Do we really want to change? The way to truly change our dilemma today is only found when we search for resolution more widely than simply situating it in the possession of an Other. As we argued earlier, in the discussion of *Mad Max*, there is no Green Land, no hope or promised land elsewhere; it lies within ourselves, where we founded our civilisation, the Earth, which will become a wasteland sooner or later if change does not happen nor operates at the level of the subject.

I am hopeful and positive that we will survive the chaos of these current times, as I truly believe in the subject's power of subversion in language and jouissance. I am convinced of this from the evidence of my constant interactions with the subject of desire and the drive (between language and jouissance) in my clinical practice on a daily basis. There is no such thing as an apocalyptic era that awaits the human race; history is patient.

To Aryamehr(s) of Iran

Bibliography

Benvenuto, S. (2016). *What Are Perversions?* London: Karnac.

Freud, S. (1913–1914). Totem and taboo. In: J. Strachey, ed., *The Standard Edition of the Complete Psychological Works of Sigmund Freud, Vol 13*, pp. 1–162. London: Vintage, 2001.

Freud, S. (1920–1922). Group psychology. In: J. Strachey, ed., *The Standard Edition of the Complete Psychological Works of Sigmund Freud, Vol XVIII*, pp. 67–143. London: Vintage, 2001.

Lacan, J. (1955–6). *The Seminar of Jacques Lacan: Book III. The Psychoses*. J.A. Miller (ed)., Russell Grigg (Trans). London: Routledge, 1993.

Lacan, J. (1963–4). *The Seminar of Jacque Lacan: Book XI: Four Fundamental Concepts of Psychoanalysis*. Alan Sheridan (Trans). New York & London: Norton.

Lacan, J. (1966). *Écrits: The Mirror stage as Formative of the I Function as Revealed in Psychoanalytic Experience*, 1949. Bruce Fink (Trans). New York & London: Norton, pp. 75–82.

Lacan, J. (1967). La Proposition du 9 octobre 1967 sur le psychanalyste de l'École. *Scilicet*, 1: 14–30. 1968.

Lacan, J. (1975–6). *Le Séminaire Livre XXIII: Le Sinthome*. Paris: Seuil.

Index

For Product Safety Concerns and Information please contact our EU
representative GPSR@taylorandfrancis.com
Taylor & Francis Verlag GmbH, Kaufingerstraße 24, 80331 München, Germany